*This book is dedicated to the idea that art is a dynamic tool in human growth
and to the art teacher who makes it possible*

UNDERSTANDING
AND
CREATING ART

UNDER
AND

BOOK ONE

STANDING CREATING ART

ERNEST GOLDSTEIN
THEODORE H. KATZ
JO D. KOWALCHUK
ROBERT SAUNDERS

West Publishing Company
St. Paul   New York   Los Angeles   San Francisco

ABOUT THE AUTHORS

Ernest Goldstein is an art critic, educator, and author of books on art, literature, and film. He is the creator of the *Let's Get Lost in a Painting* series and author of four of the books in the series: *The Gulf Stream, The Peaceable Kingdom, Washington Crossing the Delaware*, and *American Gothic*.

Theodore H. Katz, Ed.D., is an artist, administrator and teacher. He is Deputy Director for Programs at the Oregon Art Institute in Portland, Oregon and was formerly Chief of the Division of Education at the Philadelphia Museum of Art. He has developed model programs in arts education throughout the United States for school systems as diverse as New York, North Carolina, Pennsylvania and New Mexico. His numerous publications include *Museums and Schools: Partners in Teaching*.

Jo D. Kowalchuk is Program Specialist in Arts Curriculum for the Palm Beach County Schools, Palm Beach, Florida. She has taught art in Alabama, Georgia, and Florida. She served as vice president of the National Art Education Association and was on the Editorial Advisory Board of *School Arts* magazine. She is an active member of Delta Kappa Gamma International.

Robert J. Saunders, Ed.D., is Art Consultant for the Connecticut Department of Education and formerly taught art in California, New York, and New Jersey. He is the author of several books in art education including *Teaching Through Art* and *Relating Art and Humanities to the Classroom*. With Ernest Goldstein he co-authored *The Brooklyn Bridge* in the *Let's Get Lost in a Painting* series. He is a frequent contributor to art education journals.

CONTRIBUTORS

Core Activities and Annotations for
Let's Get Lost In a Painting:
  Elizabeth L. Katz and Janice Plank

Photography Activities:
  Constance J. Rudy

Printmaking and Bookmaking Activities:
  Elizabeth Kowalchuk

Craft Activities:
  Maryanne Corwin

Watercolor Activities:
  Susan Carey

Special thanks to the authors for illustration contributions.

Library of Congress Cataloging-in-Publication Data
Main entry under title:

Understanding and creating art.

  Includes bibliography and index.
  Summary: Discusses some important paintings and sculpture in terms of design elements and also from the viewpoint of the artist. Includes questions and art activities.
  1. Painting—Psychological aspects—Juvenile literature.   2. Composition (Art)—Juvenile literature.
3. Visual perception—Juvenile literature. [1. Art appreciation.   2. Composition (Art)   3. Design]
I. Goldstein, Ernest, 1933–
ND1146.U53   1985   700   85-14823
ISBN 0–314–54066–0

CONTENTS

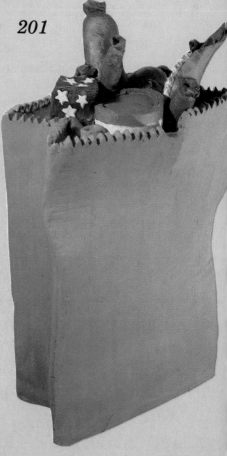

INTRODUCTION

Welcome to the world of the artist. It is a special world, not a secret world. You do not have to be an artist to be a part of it. It is enough that you enjoy art and feel that it can contribute something important to your life.

We are going to show you how artists have explored the way we see the world, and how they have changed our vision. We will show you how artists have responded to the environmental world, and to their mental world. You will read about artists in their mental world of symbols and allegories, of heroes and history, and of the industrial world of the twentieth century.

Sometimes we think the real world is the one we see and touch. For the artist, all worlds are real. They make the world of dreams, fantasy, and imagination as real for us as the one we can touch and see. They reveal a part of us to ourselves that is also a real world—the world of feelings, thoughts, and ideas.

This book is also about the problems artists solve in learning their craft and in discovering new ways of making visual illusions in order to present a truer picture of the world.

As times and people change, artists must change the way they interpret the world. We have written this book to tell you about what has been happening for hundreds of years in the world of the artist, so that it can be important to you, too, and can make your life richer and more exciting.

Besides reading about art, you will be making art, learning how to look at art, and talking about art.

So, join us in UNDERSTANDING AND CREATING ART. We hope you enjoy our book as much as we enjoyed preparing it for you. We are artists too, and we want to share our world with you.

Ernest Goldstein
Theodore H. Katz
Jo D. Kowalchuk
Robert J. Saunders

CREDITS & ACKNOWLEDGMENTS

Figures 1, 4, 7, 10, 23. (Entire painting.)

Figures 2, 5, 9, 12, 17, 24, 27. (details) Winslow Homer *The Gulf Stream*. The Metropolitan Museum of Art, New York, Wolfe Collection, 1906.

Figure 12. Winslow Homer, *Study for the Gulf Stream*. Courtesy of the Cooper-Hewitt Museum, The Smithsonian Institution, National Museum of Design.

Figure 13. The Ark and Homer's studio (formerly the stable) at Prout's Neck, ca. 1884. The Homer Collection, Bowdoin College Museum of Art, Brunswick, Maine.

Figure 14. Winslow Homer working on *The Gulf Stream* in his studio. The Homer Collection, Bowdoin College Museum of Art, Brunswick, Maine.

Figure 17. Katsushika Hokusai, *The Great Wave Off Kanagawa*. The Metropolitan Museum of Art, New York, The Howard Mansfield Collection, Rogers Fund, 1936.

Figure 18. Winslow Homer, *Shark Fishing*. Private collection, New York.

Figure 19. Winslow Homer, *Rum Cay*. Courtesy Worcester Art Museum, Worcester, Massachusetts.

Figure 20. Winslow Homer, *The Gulf Stream*. Collection of the Art Institute of Chicago.

Figure 21. John Singleton Copley, *Brook Watson and the Shark*. National Gallery of Art, Washington D.C., Ferdinand Lammont Belin Fund.

Figure 22. Winslow Homer, *The Visit of the Old Mistress*. National Museum of American Art (formerly the National Collection of Fine Arts), Smithsonian Institution (detail of the above as **Figure 23**).

Figure 25. Winslow Homer, *West Point, Prout's Neck*. Courtesy Sterling and Francine Clark Art Institute, Williamstown, Massachusetts.

Figure 28. Kuppers, Harald, *Color: Origins, Systems, Uses*. New York: Van Nostrand Reinhold Company, 1972.

Figure 29. The Color Wheel and color wheel diagram courtesy of Grumbacher Color Compass, New York, 1977 (front illustration from the 3rd edition).

Figures 30 and 31. Original drawings under the graphic direction of Marsha Cohen; re-rendered for this edition by Scott Chelius.

Figure 32. Courtesy of the Tate Gallery, London.

Figures 33 and 40. Collection of The Museum of Modern Art. Lillie P. Bliss Bequest.

Figure 34. Courtesy of The Gilcrease Museum and Institute, Tulsa, Oklahoma.

Figure 35. Courtesy Haags Gemeente museum, The Hague.

Figure 36. Courtesy Haags Gemeente museum, The Hague.

Figure 37. Courtesy Haags Gemeente museum, The Hague.

Figure 38. Courtesy of The Boston Museum of Fine Arts, Boston, Massachusetts.

Figure 39. Courtesy of Dr. Castor, 1970. Private collection.

Figure 41. Courtesy of The Cleveland Museum of Art. Gift of Mr. and Mrs. Severance A. Millikin.

Figure 42. Tokyo National Museum.

Figure 43. The Art Museum, Princeton University, Princeton, New Jersey.

Figure 44. The Art Museum, Princeton University, Princeton, New Jersey.

Figure 45. Courtesy of the Kunsthistorisches Museum, Vienna.

Figure 46. Courtesy of the Metropolitan Museum, New York. Bequest of Mrs. H.O. Havermeyer, 1929. The H.O. Havermeyer Collection.

Figure 47. Collection of The Whitney Museum of American Art, New York (photo G. Clements).

Figure 48. Courtesy The Museum of Fine Arts, Boston, Massachusetts.

Figure 49. Kunsthalle, Hamburg, West Germany.

Figure 50. Courtesy of The British Museum, London.

Figure 51. Courtesy of The Metropolitan Museum of Art, New York. Bequest of Mrs. H.O. Havermeyer, 1929. The H.O. Havermeyer Collection.

Figure 52. Courtesy of The Metropolitan Museum of Art, New York. The Fletcher Fund.

Figure 53. The Saint Louis Art Museum, museum purchase. Elizabeth McMillan Fund.

Figure 54. Museum Boymans van Beuningen, Rotterdam, The Netherlands.

Figure 55. Courtesy of the Albertina Graphics Collection, Vienna.

Figure 56. Courtesy of The Smith College Museum of Art, Northampton, Massachusetts.

Figure 57. Courtesy of the Asian Art Museum of San Francisco. The Avery Brundage Collection.

Figure 58. Courtesy of The Seattle Art Museum, Seattle, Washington.

Figure 59. Courtesy of The Asian Art Museum of San Francisco. The Avery Brundage Collection.

Figure 60. Courtesy of The Philadelphia Museum of Art. Louise and Walter Arensberg Collection.

Figure 61. Courtesy of The Museum of Modern Art, New York. Acquired through the Lillie P. Bliss Bequest.

Figure 62. Pace-McGill Collection, New York. Copyright by Robert Frank, *The Americans*, 1958.

Figure 63. Courtesy of The Library of Congress, Washington, D.C.

Figure 64. Copyright © 1980 by Barry Brukoff.

Figure 65. Courtesy of The San Francisco Museum of Modern Art. Mrs. Ferdinand C. Smith Fund purchase.

Figure 66. The Lacock Collection, The Fox Talbot Museum, Britain.

Figure 67. Courtesy of The Metropolitan Museum of Art, New York. Gift of Alfred Stieglitz, 1933.

Figure 68. Courtesy of The Art Institute of Chicago.

Figure 69. Courtesy of The Metropolitan Museum of Art, New York. David Hunter McAlpin Fund.

Figure 70. Magnum Photos, New York.

Figure 72. Victoria and Albert Museum, London.

Figure 73. Collection of The Museum of Modern Art, New York. Gift of Joseph H. Heil.

Figure 74. Private collection.

Figure 75. Courtesy Kraushaar Gallery, New York (photo by G. Clements).

Figure 76. Courtesy of The Whitney Museum of American Art, New York (Collection), photo by Sandak, Inc., Connecticut.

Figure 77. Museum Boymans van Beuningen, Rotterdam, The Netherlands.

Figure 78. Photo courtesy of The Bonington Collection, Britain.

Figures 79 and 80. Drawing by Scott Chelius.

Figure 81A. The Granger Collection, New York; **Figure B** Magnum Photos, Erich Lessing.

Figure 82. Courtesy The Navaho Museum of Ceremonial Art, Santa Fe, New Mexico.

Figure 84. The Granger Collection, New York.

Figure 85. (A) Courtesy of The British Museum, London; (B) The Pantechicon, London.

Figure 86. The Granger Collection, New York.

Figure 87. The Frick Collection, 1937. *The Temptation of Christ on the Mountain*.

Figure 88. Courtesy of The Whitney Museum of American Art, 1956 (photo by G. Clements).

Figure 89. Courtesy Chelius Design Studios.

Figures 90, 103, 113 (entire painting). **Figures 94, 95, 100** (details). All courtesy of the Art Institute of Chicago.

Figure 91. Photo copyright "This is Grant Wood Country," Joan Liffring-Zug.

Figures 92 and 93. Drawings by Marsha Cohen.

Figures 96 and 97. Drawing by Marsha Cohen.

Figure 101. *Photo of the Eldon House* by Carl E. Smith.

Figure 102. *First painting of the Eldon House.* Courtesy of Parc Rinard.

Figure 103. *Pencil sketch for American Gothic.* Courtesy of Art One Service.

Figure 105. Courtesy of Marsha Cohen.

Figure 106. Courtesy of Marsha Cohen.

Figure 107. Courtesy of Marsha Cohen.

Figure 108. Courtesy of Marsha Cohen.

Figure 109. Courtesy of The Metropolitan Museum of Art, New York. The Jules Bache Collection, 1949.

Figures 110 and 112. The Metropolitan Museum of Art, New York. The Robert Lehman Collection, 1975.

Figure 111. Art Institute of Chicago.

Figure 113. Art Institute of Chicago.

Figures 114 and 115. Collection of the Cedar Rapids Museum of Art, Cedar Rapids, Iowa.

Figure 116. The Esmark Collection of Currier and Ives.

Figure 117. Curry Sod House. Nebraska Historical Society.

Figure 118. Cincinatti Art Museum, The Edwin and Virginia Irwin Memorial. Copyright Estate of Grant Wood. Courtesy of Associated American Artist.

Figure 119. Courtesy of The Carnegie-Stout Public Library, Dubuque, Iowa.

Figure 120. Family Photograph Album, the Grant Wood Collection, Davenport Municipal Art Gallery, Davenport, Iowa.

Figure 121. Courtesy the Carnegie-Stout Public Library, Dubuque, Iowa.

Figure 122. Courtesy of the John Deere Company, Moline, Illinois.

Figure 123. Courtesy of the Muskegon Museum of Art, Muskegon, Michigan.

Figure 123. Courtesy of The Saint Louis Art Museum, Saint Louis, Missouri.

Figure 124. Courtesy Muskegon Museum of Art, Muskegon, Michigan.

Figure 125. Photo courtesy of F.L. Kenett. Copyright George Rainbird, Robert Harding Associates, London.

Figure 126. Courtesy of the Tate Gallery, London.

Figure 127. Courtesy of the Louvre, Paris, France.

Figure 128. Courtesy of The Huntington Hartford Museum, Los Angeles, California.

Figure 129. The Granger Collection, New York.

Figure 130. The National Gallery, Rome, Italy.

Figure 131. The National Museum, Paris, France.

Figure 132. The Prado Museum, Madrid, Spain.

Figure 133. Courtesy of the Wichita Art Museum, Wichita, Kansas.

Figure 134. (A) Rembrandt House, Amsterdam; (B) Mauritshuis, The Hague; (C) Kunsthistorisches Museum, Vienna.

Figure 135. Courtesy Denver Art Museum, Denver, Colorado.

Figure 136. Courtesy of Hallmark Cards, Collection and Archives.

Figure 137. Collection of Mrs. Eero Saarinen.

Figure 138. Courtesy of Christies, New York.

Figure 139. Courtesy of the National Gallery of Art, Washington, D.C. Gift of Mr. and Mrs. Robert Woods Bliss, 1949.

Figures 140 and 141. Courtesy of the Metropolitan Museum of Art, New York. Gift of Julian A. Berwind, 1953.

Figure 142. Collection of the Brandywine River Museum, Pennsylvania.

Figure 144. A Francis Stoppelman photograph.

Figure 145. Courtesy of The Brooklyn Museum.

Figure 146. "Bicyclists, Westerwald, 1922" Copyright © by Aperture, a division of Silver Mountain Foundation Inc., as published in *August Sander/The Aperture History of Photography Series*, Aperture, New York, NY, 1977.

Figure 147. "Unemployed, Cologne, 1928." Copyright © by Aperture, a division of Silver Mountain Foundation, Inc., as published in *August Sander/The Aperture History of Photography Series*, Aperture, New York, NY, 1977.

Figure 148. Courtesy of the Imogen Cunningham Trust.

Figures 149 and 150. Courtesy of The Museum of Modern Art, New York.

Figure 151. Courtesy of the Brooklyn Museum.

Figure 152. Courtesy of The Metropolitan Museum of Art, New York. Gift of Miss Georgia O'Keeffe, 1955.

Figures 153, 154, 155. The University of Nebraska, Lincoln, Nebraska.

Figure 156. Courtesy of the Philadelphia Museum of Art. Gift of Lessing J. Rosenwald.

Figures 157 and 158. Courtesy of The Philadelphia Museum of Art. Purchase the Harrison Fund.

Figure 159. (A) Collection of The Museum of Modern Art, New York. Given Anonymously; (B) Collection of The Whitney Museum of American Art, New York; (C) Collection of The Whitney Museum of American Art, New York.

Figure 160. Collection of the Museum of Modern Art, New York. Gift of Mr. and Mrs. John Polk in honor of Paul J. Sachs.

Figure 161. Courtesy of The Hirshhorn Museum and Sculpture Gardens, Washington, D.C.

Figure 162. Courtesy of the Louvre, Paris, France.

Figure 163. Courtesy of the Kupferstichkabinett Staatliche Museen, Berlin.

Figure 164. Reproduced by permission of Holt, Rinehart and Winston, Inc.

Figure 165. Chelius Design Studios.

Figure 166. Courtesy of The Granger Collection, New York.

Figure 167. Mikki Ansin, Taurus Photos, Inc., New York.

Figure 168. Courtesy of the Museé Royaux des Beaux Arts, Brussels.

Figure 169. Courtesy of The Museum of Fine Arts, Boston, Massachusetts. Gift of Quincy A. Shaw, Jr. and Mrs. Marion Shaw Houghton, 1917.

Figure 170. A Francis Stoppelman photo.

Figure 171. A Francis Stoppelman photo.

Figure 172. Courtesy of The Philadelphia Museum of Art. Gift of Wright S. Ludington.

Figure 173. Courtesy of The Philadelphia Museum of Art (photo by R. Echelmeyer).

Figure 174. Courtesy of The Metropolitan Museum of Art, New York. Given to the United States by Egypt in 1956; awarded to The Metropolitan Museum of Art in 1967; installed in the museum's Sackler wing in 1978.

Figure 175. Courtesy of The Metropolitan Museum of Art, New York. Bashford Dean Memorial Collection; funds from various donors, 1929.

Figure 176. Courtesy of The Metropolitan Museum of Art, New York. Gift of Eva Drexel Dahlgreen, 1977.

We wish to thank all those who granted permission to reproduce the artwork in this volume. Every effort was made to locate owners and secure permissions for all this art as reproduced. In the few cases where owners could not be found, upon notification, Garrard Publishing Company is prepared to properly acknowledge the owner and the use of the artwork.

THE ARTIST
AND
NATURE

UNIT 1

LET'S GET LOST IN A PAINTING

The Gulf Stream

by Winslow Homer

Did you ever look at a painting and say to yourself, "I like it. I don't know why, I just like it"? And did you ever wonder what the artist did to make you feel that way?

As you enter the world of Winslow Homer's The Gulf Stream, *you will seek answers to these questions and many others. The real fun will be in the challenge to look and find the answers yourself. They may be quite different from anyone else's. That is not important. In the end, only you will judge whether you like it—or even what it means. Before you begin, turn the page and study the painting.*

Figure 1. *The Gulf Stream* **by Winslow Homer (1899). (Pages 4–5)**

PAINTING A STORY

What's happening here? A storm, a shipwreck, and hungry sharks waiting for a human meal. But the sharks are not really waiting; one of them is trying to jump into the boat. That big one in front with the scary eye and jaws full of terrible teeth wants to leap right out of the picture and bite the viewer.

The ocean is full of sharks. How many do you see in the painting? Count them! One. . . two. . . three . . . maybe four or five? A hundred beneath the water possibly? Try again. That big one in front—is that his tail in the lower right corner? Or are there two different sharks? How can you tell? Place your finger on the head and trace the line into the water back to the tail. Still not sure? The artist wants you to think there are many sharks. Even when the artist plays tricks with your eyesight, the answer is there. Some detective work is needed.

Figure 2. Detail of *The Gulf Stream*.

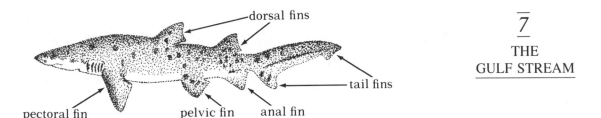

Figure 3. Shark fins.

The clue is in the fins. Look at the illustration and study the different kinds of shark fins.

Now go back to that big shark in the front. The fins on top separated by the water are the dorsal fins. Below and near the mouth you can almost make out the pectoral fin. In the water is the pelvic fin, followed by the anal fin and the big lopsided tail swishing red spray.

There is one shark in front. A second shark is near the boat, again separated by the water. Can you name the big fin almost touching the cabin? You are right if you called it the pectoral. There is another pectoral fin—of a third shark! You know what it is because the shape is the same as the large pectoral fin of the shark near the boat. Now can you see the three sharks? Before reading on, try making your own sketch of them in the water. Which way are they moving? The illustration shown here is likely what the artist had in mind.

If your eye is really sharp, you can even tell the kind of shark. Find the tail of the shark near the boat. Trace the line of the fin and you will come to a funny hitch. That hitch is the mark of a sand shark—that and the round, pointed snout.

Now that you know the number of sharks you might ask, "So what?" What does it tell you about the painting? The answer is not in what you see, but how you look. You get the feeling of an ocean full of monsters. Yet, there are only three. Looking at a painting is like solving a puzzle. The artist has given the clues. Now you must find them.

If the sharks do not get the man, there is still more danger out there. Look at the ocean! The water is rough and the waves are high. In the right rear corner there is more trouble. Big trouble! A waterspout! A waterspout is a tor-

Figure 4. Outline of sharks in *The Gulf Stream*.

Figure 5. Detail of the waterspout in *The Gulf Stream*.

nado on the water. Sailors have a very simple rule about them: DANGER, get away fast! That sailing ship on the left-hand side got the message. It is at full sail going as fast and as far away as possible.

Do you think the storm is coming toward the man in the boat, or has it already gone by? Waterspouts are tricky and follow no one direction. How can you tell, or *can* you tell? The boat tells a lot. A bowsprit is the large pole that holds the sail. Here, the bowsprit is broken. Sails are hanging over the boat and the rudder is gone. The boat is helpless, out of control and drifting. The man and his boat have been through a storm—perhaps caused by the waterspout.

Waterspouts are common in the Gulf Stream. Now, how do you know it is the Gulf Stream? Even if you do not know the title, the artist gives clues. First, the name of the boat painted on the back is *Anne of Key West*. Key West is at the tip of Florida. Second, sand sharks and flying fish—those specks of white to the right of the boat—are found in the Gulf Stream off the coast of Florida. Third, the Gulf Stream is marked by deep blue water that is much bluer than the ocean around it.

Winslow Homer finished painting *The Gulf Stream* in 1899. The date is in black at the lower left corner. From the very first time it was shown, people have been frightened by it. It is called a dramatic painting because you can "read" it like a drama or story—a horror story!

If the sharks or the storm do not get the man, there is still trouble. The boat could plow into a reef. That big white curlicue behind the boat may be caused by waves crashing over a coral reef. Or again, all alone, deserted by the only possible help—a ship going the other way—with no food or water, the man could starve to death. So, his end could be near. Anyway, that is what you see at first glance, and that is what everyone has always seen, a frightening picture.

When the painting was first shown in a museum, a group of confused people wrote to Winslow Homer and asked him to explain what he meant. Homer gave the following answer: "The sharks and the boat are not important to the picture. They have been blown out to sea by a hurricane. The man on the boat, who seems so hot and dazed, will be rescued and live happily ever after."

What a strange thing to say! Naturally, nobody believed him then, and to this day, people continue to think the worst. How is a happy ending possible when death seems so close? The man is at the mercy of Mother Nature, who does not seem to care. The ocean can be cruel—very cruel.

Why do people love a painting that gives them the chills? Homer said that the man will live happily ever after. Perhaps he was kidding—but maybe he wasn't. Remember, his letter said that the sharks and the boat were not important to the picture. So, what is the story about? When a great artist does a dramatic painting, he does not give you the whole story. He selects one moment, one special moment when time stands still on the canvas. It is the moment that puts you inside and tells everything—what happened and what will happen. Now, go back and find that moment.

Figure 6. Map of the Gulf Stream and the Keys islands off the tip of Florida.

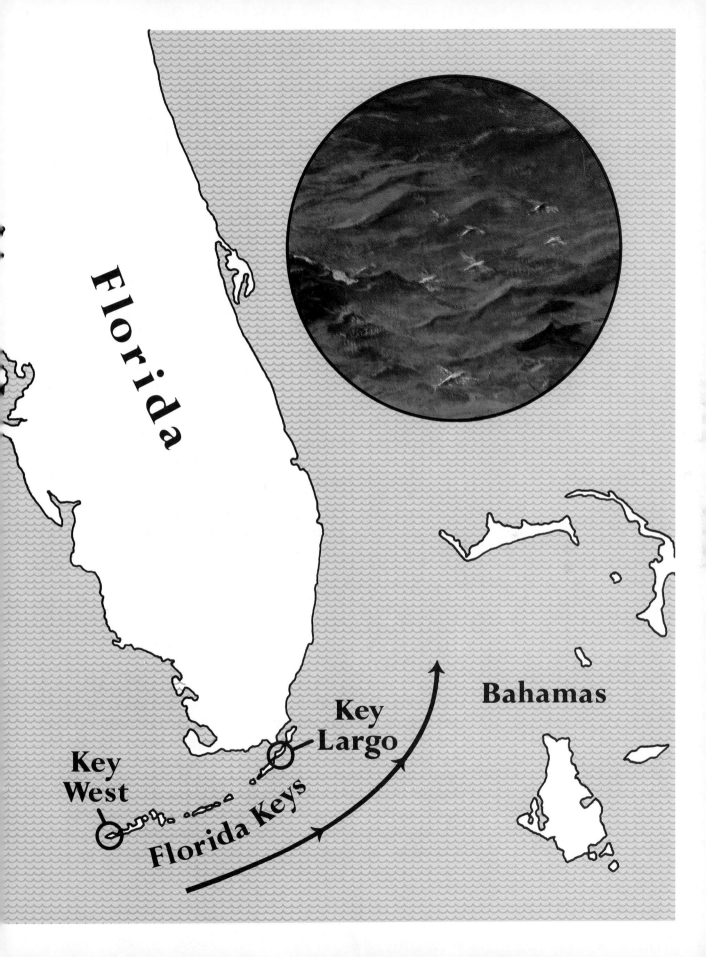

COLOR AND LIGHT

If the ocean has danger, it also has great beauty. A viewer once told another famous English ocean painter that she had never seen the colors of the water that he had put in his painting. The artist, J. M. Turner responded, "Ah, but don't you wish you could?" And that's the same feeling you get from the blues, blue greens, violets, sapphires, and emeralds of *The Gulf Stream*.

Try to imagine where the sun is. You say it is not there? But it is. Sunlight is falling directly on the boat. Homer shows the position of the sun by means of shadow and color. If you wanted to discover that position through shadows, here is one possible solution. Study the diagram (Figure 7) for help. You can see the shadow on the sugarcane, the man, and the mast. The shadow on the sugarcane falls at an angle. If a line is drawn from the cane to the cabin cover, it moves up to the right. The shadows on the man point to the light overhead. When you line up these shadows with the mast, they all line up above his head. The sun is straight above.

Homer's use of brown is another clue to the position of the sun. There are dark browns, almost in shadow, on the side of the cabin and lower left side of the boat. There are sunny white browns on the upper part of the deck and pink-and-white browns on top of the cabin and on the sailor's skin. If you go to the Metropolitan Museum of Art in New York City and see the original painting, get close to it. You will see how much variety Homer put into his browns.

Homer knew the laws of color and understood that the best way to contrast the rich variety of browns was by the use of black and white. He often said that the proper use of black and white can suggest color. Now look at the shades of white. The tropical sun overhead is very strong. It is so hot that you can see white beads of perspiration on the man's dark skin. Direct sunlight is falling on the warm whites of the sail, on the man's body, pants, and on the lower corner of the boat. The white becomes less bright when it is picked up on the flying fish and the sharks. Toward the waterspout the white looks cold, like the green of the crashing waves. Notice the solid white line between the blue-gray waterspout and the sailing ship. At first, the white border seems like the horizon, but it is not. It is probably foam coming off the waves whipped up by the winds of the storm. As your

Figure 7. Lines point to the sun located directly above the sailor.

eyes pass the sailing ship to the left and return to the center
of the picture, you can again pick up direct sunlight with
flecks of warm white dancing on top of the waves.

Figure 8. Notice how Homer used white to indicate sunlight and sea foam.

The color in *The Gulf Stream* is one of the glories of American art—an achievement! A boat of brown is lightened by black and darkened by white against the rich blues of the sea. The blues are darkened at the crests of the waves and lightened by direct sunlight. The more you look, the more color you see. All that beauty should not have an unhappy ending.

That is what you see, but what does the painting say? What is all that red stuff in the water? Could it be blood? Is the man alone because another friend was thrown overboard? It looks like blood, but it is not. It is seaweed. Red seaweed comes into the Gulf Stream from the Gulf of Mexico. In this case it could have been dug up by the storm. On the other hand, there is that big open gash close to the mouth of the big shark. Mysterious—and frightening! Homer might have put it there to give a feeling of violence.

THE DRAMA WITHIN AND WITHOUT

If all these terrible things might be happening to the man on the boat, how do you think he feels? What is going on inside his mind? Take another look, a very careful look! Read his face. Does he have the look of a man who has lost a battle? Does he seem frightened? Scared? Angry? Determined? Or just waiting for something to happen? Can you really tell?

Figure 9. Detail from *The Gulf Stream* shows the look of determination in the man's face.

Figure 10. Arrows indicate the movement in *The Gulf Stream*.

A famous writer looked at the picture for a long time and came up with this idea: "The important point of this story is the man's distance from a shore or even a safe place. The man is still alive, but not for long. The picture is designed like a big trap ready to close. On one side of the trap are the sharks and on the other side, the waterspout. The man has not only lost the battle, but does not even have any strength left to call for help from the other ship. Even if he escapes these dangers around him, he will probably starve from lack of food and water."

Do you agree? Is that what you see on the man's face? Take another look. What can you tell about him? He is very strong. From the way he is sitting, you can see the great strength in his arms and chest. The body is relaxed and he is resting on one elbow.

Notice how the artist has turned his head. From this position you can see determination in the powerful neck.

And he is looking straight out to the side. That tells a lot. If he were a beaten man, a defeated man, he would be looking down. If he were looking up, he might be either desperate and praying to the heavens, or sure that help was coming. But the man is looking to the side! Whatever he is looking at, whatever he is thinking, remains a mystery. What you do know is that this is not the look of someone who has given up the battle.

Another reason Homer may have painted the man leaning and looking to the right is because he wanted you to look in that direction. If you do, you will see the flying fish which point to the waterspout. The waterspout leans toward the left—toward the sailing ship. The ship directs the eye back into the painting—back to the man. Which way do the sharks and the boat direct you to look? The big shark points left—but its fin points up right. The smaller shark points right. In a painting this is called "movement." The drawing below shows the movement in the painting.

THE BOAT

This man has been in trouble before, and perhaps in these very same waters. How can you know that? More detective work. How about the boat? What kind is it? A sailboat! But what kind of sailboat? You might say, "What difference does it make? A boat is a boat." Not so. In this case, the sailboat is

Figure 11. The boat as it might have looked before the storm.

a very special kind. A smack boat sloop. Smack boats have a well or hole between the cabin and hatch to keep the fish. The illustration (Figure 11) shows what the boat looked like before the storm, safe in the harbor. You can see all the fishing gear on the boat: fish pots, water barrels, nets, and conch shells.

Although these boats are no longer in use, they are part of the American heritage. Like the boat in the picture, they looked more like a tub. They were workboats, and the men who sailed them were always on the water.

There is a wonderful tradition about the brave sailors who worked on these boats around the Gulf Stream. These men were known for their strength and courage. They worked on the ocean day and night, year after year, and often went to sea in bad weather. The smack boat sailor was a great sailor. It was said that he could smell bad weather. He could read the clouds for signs of land beyond the horizon. He could even steer his boat by the formations of grass and coral in the seabed when out of sight of land.

The man in the painting was this kind of sailor. Now, one more look at his face and what do you see? Does *he* think he will make it? He has strength and courage. What else does the sailor have? Remember the sugarcane in his right hand? So he is not going to starve because sugarcane offers both food and water. His eyes could be on those flying fish and maybe, just maybe, he will catch a few. And, of course, it is possible that he may have some fish in the well.

Now can you figure out if the boat is sinking? Again, Homer gave the answer. Put your finger on the corner of the stern, or the back end. Trace the edge of the boat, including the space hidden by the shark. The line of the boat is above the water. It is not taking on water. In sailors' language, the ship still has "integrity." This is the position Homer wanted. Compare it to an earlier study of *The Gulf Stream* (Figure 12). In this work the boat is taking on water. In the final picture it is not clear. Although it is helpless and tipping it is not sinking, yet.

In fact there are several problems in this picture that are not clear. For example, sharks never come to the top of the water during a storm. They stay far below. The water is rough, but it still might not be made so by the waterspout. Now things really get tough. Homer knew sharks and he

Figure 12. Compare the boat in the inset to an earlier version of *The Gulf Stream*.

knew that the sand shark does not attack human beings. In a frenzy, however, sharks attack anything, and there is that big gash on the shark's mouth. So you still really do not know what is going on.

Homer's letter said there was something else. Another story. In fact there are two dramas. The first one is outside the man—on the ocean. The second one, inside the man, begins with his relaxed position and the bold look on his face. What you think might happen changes the moment you are inside the painting. Now the question becomes: What does *he* think will happen? What is on the sailor's mind? Or another way—what was on Homer's mind? For that answer you must go to the history of this artist and how he did his work.

THE ARTIST

Winslow Homer was born in Boston in 1826 and died in Prouts Neck, Maine, in 1910. During his lifetime he had become the outstanding artist of the American outdoors. His paintings of hunting scenes in the Adirondacks, fishermen on dories, and waves smashing against the rocky coast of Maine are now part of the American heritage. When the Metropolitan Museum of Art in New York City bought *The Gulf Stream*, it paid him the highest amount he ever received for a painting, $4,500—a great sum of money in those days.

Homer was a man who liked to be alone. And so, to this day, very little is known about him. He lived like a pioneer. At the age of forty, he left city life and moved to the lonely ocean village of Prouts Neck, Maine. He kept away from people, even art critics and buyers, and talked to no one about himself or his work.

When Homer was quite old, the writer William Howe Downes asked him for information for a biography. Homer answered: "I think that it would probably kill me to have such a thing appear, and as the most interesting part of my life is of no concern to the public, I must decline."

This was not Homer's first refusal. In the letter about the meaning of *The Gulf Stream*, he had written the following thought: "You ask me for a full description of my picture *The Gulf Stream*. I regret very much that I have painted a picture that *requires* any description." But the meaning is not clear and the picture does require "description." There

Figure 13. Winslow Homer's home at Prouts Neck, Maine. The smaller building to the left was his studio.

are two valuable clues outside this work. For help you can go to his other paintings and to some important events during his lifetime.

You can start your detective work with a photograph. There is only one photograph of Homer in his studio. He is standing in front of *The Gulf Stream*. How big do you think the painting is? Here is a clue: Homer was approximately five feet six inches tall. The painting is twenty-eight by forty-nine inches. If you measure a rectangle on the floor, you can get the size of the real painting. That photograph

Figure 14. Homer in his studio at work on *The Gulf Stream*.

tells you much. You can see that the painting is unfinished. In the background it is possible to make out two waterspouts. There is still no white spray over the tail, and the waves are not fully painted.

How long does it take to finish a painting? When did Homer know that the work was done—that the color, design, and idea all fit together? He started *The Gulf Stream* in 1897, and finished it in 1899—two years later. During those two years the painting was shown and returned to him for more changes. Why? Even after he worked out the details, Homer considered the painting a failure if the viewer did not understand the idea. His work was not simply a photograph of what he saw, but rather his way of expressing feelings and ideas. At that time people did not understand what he was trying to do.

Today viewers consider the painting "great." You can look at it time and again and always find something new—a little detail, not seen before, to add to your pleasure. For example, sharks really do not have teeth like the ones in the painting. But who cares? When the shark opens its mouth, you see jaws but Homer painted *maw*s. MAWS, now that is a word! *Maws* means "appetite" in a very special sense—the appetite of a wild, man-eating creature. And that is what you see and feel—the appetite of a shark too close to the man in the boat, ready to swallow the victim whole.

The ability to describe a thing and give it such powerful feelings is the inspiration of the artist. This was Homer's gift: to describe and to communicate with feeling. If you use your imagination, you can see how he gives feeling to the shape of the ocean. Once he puts terror into his picture, the whole design cries out "Danger!" The illustrations (Figures

Figure 15. Notice how the image of the shark is repeated in the upper half of the painting.

Figure 16. Another image of the shark devouring the boat is shown here.

15 and 16) show how the frightening image of the shark repeats itself in the design. In the first illustration, the water forms a pattern of the huge fish with its tail as the waterspout. In the second illustration, the lines of the big waves meet to form one large, terrifying shark with the boat in its maws. The design becomes one shape—one emotion—one overpowering feeling—TERROR!

INFLUENCE OF OTHER ARTISTS

It is likely that Homer had seen that technique used before. In 1854, Admiral Perry made his famous trip to Japan and opened its ports to the world. Soon after, sailors brought back art prints of the Japanese masters. America and Europe suddenly discovered Japanese art. Hokusai was one of the greatest of the Japanese artists. Homer knew his picture *The Great Wave Off Kanagawa* (page 25). In the illustration you can see the same lacy lines of the waves.

Hokusai's large wave rolls over into curlicues—much like Homer's design of the reef. The technique is Japanese, a pretty ornament on top of the water. Hokusai's wave looks like a monster reaching out over the men in the boats, like Homer's wave, ready to swallow up the sailor. But it is remarkable that in the center of both works there is such a quiet feeling. In Hokusai's a peaceful Mount Fuji; and in Homer's the relaxed body of the man.

Figure 17. Compare Homer's wave (inset) with the curling waves in *The Great Wave Off Kanagawa* by Hokusai.

The Gulf Stream was not the first time Homer had painted sharks. He first went to the Bahamas in 1885 and soon after did a watercolor called *Shark Fishing* (page 26). Notice the power of the man using only a small line to battle the monster. Homer's watercolors and paintings of the tropics are remarkable for their strong colors and dramatic stories of man's war with nature. His pictures have no pity for man or beast. Now look at two more works: *Rum Cay* and an early study of *The Gulf Stream* (page 27).

The watercolor *Rum Cay* tells a brutal story. Look at the strength of the man: the powerful head, the huge chest, the whole body excitedly bent toward one object—the turtle. The turtle is going to lose. In 1899, Homer painted a watercolor which he also named *The Gulf Stream*. Notice that the lower side of the boat is almost in the water, while the man is high above the cabin with his shirt on. These earlier

Figure 18. *Shark Fishing* **by Winslow Homer, painted several years before** *The Gulf Stream.*

Figure 19. *Rum Cay*, another watercolor by Homer showing a
dramatic scene from the Bahamas.
Figure 20. An earlier version of *The Gulf Stream*.

works can be considered the beginning of a drama not finished until 1899 in *The Gulf Stream.*

The first shark Winslow Homer saw could have been in *Brook Watson and the Shark* (1778) by John Singleton Copley (page 29). Homer grew up around Boston. When he was very young, his parents knew how well he could draw. They also knew it was very important for him to see the work of other artists. Since *Brook Watson and the Shark* hung in the Boston Athenaeum, it is possible that young Winslow saw it many times. *The Gulf Stream* and Copley's painting are somewhat alike. Copley placed the shark right in front, leaping out of the water. Homer's shark has the same huge mouth and knife-sharp teeth as Copley's. In both pictures the shark has a frightening eye that seems almost human. But you can find something even more interesting in comparing the two: look at the faces of the men in Copley's painting. They are all frightened and upset, except one man in the center. There stands a black sailor, calm, confident, and strong before the danger.

There is something else about the Copley work that Homer knew. Brook Watson, the man in the water, had been attacked by a shark. But there was a happy ending after his terrible adventure. Later, Watson became Lord Mayor of London and paid Copley to paint his attack by the shark. Maybe this is what Homer meant when he said *The Gulf Stream* had a happy ending.

Homer had an uneasy feeling about *The Gulf Stream.* Before he finished, he wrote to his agent that he did not want "the public to poke its nose into the picture." Homer knew his people. That same public was not used to seeing such terror in paintings. He was sure people would get the wrong idea, and they did. Over the years he had painted fishermen catching sharks. When the audience first saw *The Gulf Stream*, many people said, "Now it is the shark's turn to catch the fisherman."

THE PUBLIC RESPONSE

At the first showing of *The Gulf Stream*, the critics were divided in their reports. One writer was shocked by such an awful subject. Another could not understand why "the ship was not wet with seawater" or "how the man kept himself from sliding down the boat." This last critic looked at the painting as if it were a photograph. He missed the idea in every way. With time, these kinds of questions have been answered. But there are other questions about the painting that still deserve attention. Here is one: Does it make any difference to the picture or to the story if the man is white or black? There is no one answer.

Figure 21. *Brook Watson and the Shark* **by John Singleton Copley (1778).**

This question was often asked in a different way: Why did Homer put a black man on the boat? What a sad question, sad because of the date—1899! The Civil War had ended in 1865. Thirty-four years had passed. It is sad because the fight for equal rights in art had not ended. Most paintings treated blacks as objects only, not as people. The Copley painting was the great exception. Before the Civil War, most paintings of blacks showed them either suffering in slavery, happily dancing, or playing banjos. Now, Homer puts his man in a boat in the middle of the ocean at the center of his picture. And what a magnificent human being he is! This man is not a slave. What appears at first glance to be a ball and chain on his left is an illusion. The left hand is hooked in the belt loop of his pants.

Do you think it makes any difference to the story if the man is black or white? Maybe, but no one is sure. Did it make any difference to Homer? The artist cannot lie! A great work of art is one man's way of telling the truth. There is always a reason for his choice of color, although you may never fully understand it. There are two events, however, in Homer's lifetime that tell a lot about his sense of color. They are the Civil War and the publicaton of a remarkable book, *The Laws of Contrast of Colour* by M.E. Chevreul.

AN IMPORTANT LESSON

During the Civil War, Homer was a war artist for *Harper's* magazine. He made several trips to the war front and sometimes he saw the fighting. At the front, he made sketches and then came back to New York to finish the drawings. He was what is now called an artist-reporter.

In 1875, ten years after the Civil War had ended, Homer made a trip to Petersburg, Virginia. That year is important not only in the life of the artist, but also in the history of American painting. Homer had been to Petersburg before, in 1865, after a terrible battle. He went back in 1875 and decided to live in the black neighborhood and paint. The war had been over for a long time, but there was still hate. Some white troublemakers from Petersburg were angry. Homer paid no attention. One day, a group of toughs decided to get him and drive him out of town. One rough-looking fellow came up and threatened him. Homer said, "I looked him in the eyes, as mother told us to look at a wild cow," and the man ran away. Homer did not know what happened. But a Texan, who had hidden under the porch, explained that he ran because he thought Homer had a gun in each hand and was ready to shoot him. After that, no one bothered him again. He painted a whole series of works showing blacks as black Americans—at work, in church, at play—no different from white Americans except for the color of their skin.

During his time in Petersburg, Homer painted *The Visit of the Old Mistress*. The mistress has come back to visit with the ex-slaves. What did she expect to find? What does her face tell you? She seems confused because she is not getting the friendship that she might have wanted. What do you see in the faces of the black women? Look closely at the eyes and mouths of the ex-slaves. You can see dignity, but also scorn. What do you see on the face of the large black woman in the middle? Does her look remind you of one you have seen somewhere else? Compare her face with that of the man in *The Gulf Stream*, and decide for yourself.

Figure 22. Homer's *The Visit of the Old Mistress*.

THE ARTIST AT WORK

In the lower left corner of *The Gulf Stream* are the date and the signature of the artist in black. From our earlier study, you know how Homer used black and white to contrast color. To paint rich colors of *The Gulf Stream*, a man could spend a lifetime: first in seeing such beauty and then putting it on canvas for others to enjoy. Sometimes the work was slow and tiring. After *West Point, Prouts Neck* (Figure 25), Homer described his technique. "The picture is painted *fifteen minutes after sunset*—not one minute before—since up to that minute the clouds would have their edges lighted with a brilliant glow of color—but now, in this picture, the sun has gone beyond their range and they are in shadow. The light is from the sky in this picture. You can see that it took many days of careful study to get this effect with the sea and tide just right."

Anytime you see his work you can study color and shadow and always figure out the time of day. He once said about a picture he was painting, "I work hard every afternoon from 4:30 to 4:40 (ten minutes), that being the limit of the light in the picture."

Besides those ten minutes, Homer spent hours and years studying the effects of sunlight on color. You might ask how he knew that the colors he saw were true. A little more detective work!

Figure 23. The face of the central figure in *The Visit of the Old Mistress.*

Figure 24. Compare the woman's face with the face of the man in the detail from *The Gulf Stream*.

Figure 23.

Figure 24.

Homer kept a book which he read and reread. He once even called it "my bible." That book was M. E. Chevreul's *Laws of Contrast of Colour*. Chevreul, a French scientist, published his work in 1839. It was translated into English in 1858. Ever since the book appeared, it has influenced everything from housing to flower arrangement and furniture. By reading Chevreul's experiments, artists had a guide to study the sun's effects on light and color.

Homer had mastered Chevreul's laws. He knew that every object brightens if placed against a shadow. He understood how black makes brown look light, or blue look dark.

Now, go back again and see how Homer used Chevreul's law of color contrast. Brown is a dark color; blue a light one. Find the black in the painting. You see it in the empty space in the cabin and in the hatch, on the man's head, on the bottom of his pants, and around the dark border of the boat.

Figure 25. *West Point, Prouts Neck* **shows Homer's dedication to capturing the colors and beauty of the moment.**

Within the boat, the dark browns get lighter, while outside the boat the light blues get darker. In art that is called depth of color. The effects are surprising because the more you look, the more shades of colors you will find.

An artist once asked Homer if he changed the colors he saw. Homer, shocked by the question, answered, "Never, never. When I have selected a thing, I paint it exactly as it appears." Then he added something interesting: "Of course, you must not paint everything you see. You must wait, and wait patiently, for the wonderful to come and hope to have the sense to see it."

Figure 26. Note how Homer contrasted dark and light areas to highlight objects in the painting. (1885)

Waiting patiently is one way of describing Homer's life and work. His house at Prouts Neck was right on the ocean. From his window, he could study the waves rolling in against the coast, sending off sprays of light and color. He even built a "paint house" that he could move close to the ocean in a storm. His only interest was his work.

Another artist tells a story of his visit to Homer. A storm had come up and Homer said they had to see it—at once! "During my visit, a storm swept the coast. No one at Prouts Neck, not even the oldest people, could remember such bad weather. The wind blew a gale. The rain was heavy. There were clouds of mist over the rocks and the sound of the ocean rose over the waves." Homer was excited. They put on raincoats and walked along the shore. They had to hold on to the rocks, or the wind would have knocked them down. Homer watched the clouds for a change in the weather. It was for this moment that he had waited. For this he was always ready, with his paintbrush in his hand. For these moments Homer lived and remained alone.

TAKE A LAST LOOK

There is no one answer to the question of why the man in the boat is black. Homer saw a lone black sailor in a Bahamian sloop and painted him. But a Winslow Homer work includes his genius, his life, and his vision. Homer's vision opens the eye to the visual splendor in nature, and it challenges the mind to understand this man. This black American is an example of people who have faced danger before and have survived.

You still don't know what will happen to the sailor. Take one more look and figure out which way the boat is drifting. Beneath the broken mast a rope hangs in the water. It seems to be fastened to something below the wave, perhaps a sea anchor. Although hidden from view, something there is almost pulling the boat, or even guiding it. The boat is moving between the waves and the storm into the beautiful, blue water. Perhaps into safety? Something unknown is directing it. But what?

You do not know because Homer did not want you to. Perhaps he himself did not know.

You went against the artist's wish and poked your nose into his painting. You went looking for the moment that would give you the key to the puzzle. And what did you find?

Figure 27. Detail shows rope leading to something hidden from view.

Another puzzle! Although you still do not know the ending, you do know that it will be different from what you had expected.

When you are led to expect one thing and something else happens, that is called "irony." It would be visual irony if the beautiful ocean were to destroy the brave sailor. It would be dramatic irony if he were close to land and could not reach it.

But there are other ironies in this masterpiece. There is the irony of the Gulf Stream itself. In Homer's time, very little was known about "the river of blue." Ponce de Leon, the Spanish explorer, first described it; sailors navigated it; and scientists—even Benjamin Franklin, made charts of the currents. But in spite of all the effort and study, the Gulf Stream remained a mystery. Very little was known about where it began and ended, or what part it played in the ocean's flow. It is an irony that people try so hard to understand and still know so little about the Gulf Stream, the end of the story, or life itself for that matter. Like the mystery in the boat we, too, do not know the future.

It is now many years later. *The Gulf Stream* hangs in the Metropolitan Museum, and still haunts the viewer. So why do people love this painting even as it chills them and makes the future as scary as the eye of the shark?

The answer to this question is the key to the mystery. The horror is there. And yet one man's calm and courage give to the work a strength and dignity—and perhaps even faith. He is alone against the elements, but not defeated.

Like the man in the boat, Homer was alone. We are all alone, black and white, when the real trouble comes; when the monsters come out of the deep into our dreams. Alone when the world closes in on us; alone—adrift in currents of doubts, fearful about tomorrow. But that sailor knows something. Whatever it is, he is strong enough to look away from terror. In his look is the final irony. Homer was able to scare everyone who looked at *The Gulf Stream*. Everyone except the one man who could not be frightened—the man in the boat.

And who is that man in the boat? He is every one of us.

Summary Questions

1. Artists often paint people in relation to nature. Sometimes they show people enjoying nature, playing or working in natural settings, or struggling against nature's forces. After reading about Winslow Homer's *The Gulf Stream*, which type of painting do you think this is? What are the different natural forces which threaten the man in the boat?

2. Many people think the man in *The Gulf Stream* will come to an unhappy end. Can you make an argument for their reasons?

3. Why is it said that *The Gulf Stream* has "great depth of color"?

4. How did Homer use M. E. Chevreul's law of color contrast?

5. How did Homer move the viewer's eye from place to place in *The Gulf Stream*?

6. You read about some ways in which *The Gulf Stream* and John Singleton Copley's painting *Brook Watson and the Shark* are alike. What are some ways in which the two paintings are different?

7. In what way was Homer's home in Prouts Neck, Maine, important to his work?

8. Look carefully at the picture of *The Great Wave Off Kanagawa* by Hokusai (page 25). How does this show the struggle of people against natural forces? How are the fishermen in the boats struggling against nature? Are these fishermen in more or less immediate danger than the man in *The Gulf Stream*? What details in the two paintings helped you to come to your conclusion?

In the art activities sections students will be using many different types of materials.

This caution symbol is placed throughout the book next to activities in which materials are used which contain chemicals or other ingredients that may be hazardous to students. These materials should **not** be used by students without supervision by teachers. Students should be instructed to consult the teacher before proceeding with any activity which has this caution label next to it.

This caution label also refers to the proper handling of instruments, such as knives, scissors, etc.

ELEMENTS
OF
DESIGN

Look back at the painting of *The Gulf Stream* (pages 4-5). This time try to see it not as a picture of a man in a boat, but as *colors, values, forms* and *shapes, space, lines,* and *textures.* These are called the *elements* of design. An element is something that is fundamental or essential. So the elements of color, form, texture, line, space, and value are fundamental to all works of art. Artists may use these elements in different ways and in varying degrees, but an artist cannot create art without them.

Where do the elements of design come from? Look around you! Just as the images in *The Gulf Stream* came from nature, the elements of design came from Homer's visual environment. In other words, the elements of design are found in nature or in the environments that people create.

COLOR AND VALUE

Color is an important part of our world. There is color in everything we see. In 1704 the English scientist Sir Isaac Newton found that all the colors of the rainbow are contained in white light, such as sunlight. When white light passes through a prism, a band of colors is formed. This band is called a spectrum. If, after a storm, sunlight passes through nature's prism of raindrops, you can see this spectrum in the form of a rainbow.

Newton also invented the color wheel. He put the three primary colors—red, yellow, blue—and the three secondary colors—orange, green, violet—in the outer circle. Notice that the color wheel on page 41 has six other colors on the

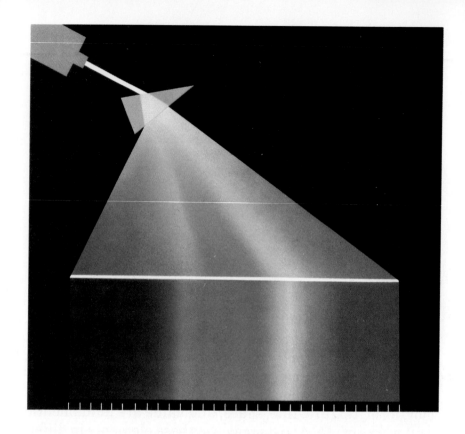

Figure 28. The prism breaks up the white light rays into a spectrum of color.

outer circle of the wheel. These are called intermediate colors because they come between the primary and secondary colors. The diagram on page 41 explains the primary, secondary, and intermediate colors and how they are mixed. Black is the sum of all colors. White is the absence of all colors, so it is not shown on the colors wheel.

As you have read, Winslow Homer is known for his use of color. Just look at the variety of blues, greens, and violets he used in the water of *The Gulf Stream*. Homer also used different values of colors. Notice the darker colors in the wave in front of the boat, and in the shadows in the wave breaking behind the boat. Can you find the lighter blue-greens where the sun shines on the water?

Activity 1 - Color   Homer used color in an exciting and dramatic way in *The Gulf Stream*. Spend a few moments looking at the painting. Note the colors in the water. How many different shades of blue do you find? Did Homer use

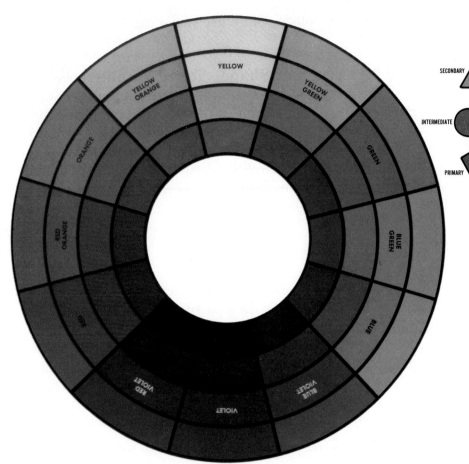

Figure 29. The color wheel shows the basic colors and the gradations between them. (*Courtesy M. Grumbacher, Inc.*)

PRIMARY COLORS

An imaginary equilateral triangle (solid line in illustration below) placed on a color circle so that one point of the triangle is at yellow, will locate the remaining two primary colors (red and blue) at the other two points.

SECONDARY COLORS

Orange, violet and green are the secondary colors. Each is placed between the two primaries that are mixed to produce it. The secondaries may be located on the color wheel by an inverted triangle (dotted line) as illustrated.

INTERMEDIATE COLORS

All the additional hues which fall between the primary and secondary colors around the color circle are known as intermediate colors and can be produced by the mixture of adjoining primary and secondary colors.

pure color? Did he use mixtures? Are the tints of the same value? Using a small amount of paint, see if you can achieve a near match to any of Homer's blues. What colors will you need to have in addition to blue? (See Figure 30.)

FORM AND SHAPE

Form is the three-dimensional feeling of an object. Shapes look flat and two-dimensional. In *The Gulf Stream,* Homer developed the solidness, or volume, of the smack boat, the man, and the sharks by giving them form. He did this by using highlights on one side of each object and shading or shadows on the opposite side. The water has volume and form because of the light and shadow in the low area between the waves, but the ship and waterspout on the horizon are just shapes. They are too far away for you to see their form, volume, or colors. They are just gray shapes in the mist.

Activity 2 - Form and Shape   To see the difference between shape and form find a three-dimensional object such as a plastic cup, apple, orange, ball, tube, or box. Make two drawings of the object. First, make an outline drawing in which you only show the shape. Next to it on the same paper, make another outline drawing of the object and then add shading to create form. Study the objects very carefully. Does your shaded object have form?

SPACE

Space is the void between solid objects and shapes. It is everywhere, all around us. In a painting it is limited to the edges of the canvas. In a painting, space can also be positive shapes. It is not always easy to figure out what is the space in a painting. In *The Gulf Stream* Homer created space around the man in the boat by placing a wave in front of him and the wave breaking behind him. He created an even greater space by putting the ship and waterspout on the horizon.

Activity 3 - Space   Cover the ship and waterspout in *The Gulf Stream* with your hands. Then take your hands away. Does the horizon look farther away with or without them? Consider the space between the ship and waterspout. Imagine them closer together. What does that do to the illusion of space that Homer tries to create? How would the effect of space in the painting change if the ship and waterspout were not in the picture? Discuss these differences in class and justify your opinion.

LINE

Artists create lines with pencils, pens, chalk, brushes, and many other tools. Lines define and enclose space. In an illustration a line may represent an actual line. It may also represent a three-dimensional form such as a building or a person. Do you remember how Homer used line in *The Gulf Stream*? Turn back to the diagram on page 16 to see the shapes that Homer's lines defined. Notice how these lines help create movement in the painting.

Activity 4 - Line   To do a diagram of the painting, take a piece of clear plastic paper about the same size as the reproduction of *The Gulf Stream*. Place it over the reproduction. Using a grease pencil, carefully diagram the most important lines you can see. Next, remove the diagram, place it over a blank paper, and look at it. What kinds of lines do you find? Are they repeated anywhere else? Which of the terms below best describe the lines in your diagram?

mechanical	static	dynamic	curved
converging	flowing	restful	
vertical	horizontal	short	
long	active	diagonal	

TEXTURE

The way things feel is their texture. A sculptor often chooses a material for its texture or the sensation of touch it offers. A painter can give us a visual experience with texture. Homer studied and observed natural textures so he could use them in his paintngs. Notice the different textures Homer used to show the water, the deck of the boat, the man's flesh, and his trousers in *The Gulf Stream*.

Activity 5 - Texture   You can produce the appearance of texture in your art work. One way to achieve texture is to do rubbings. Look around your classroom and find a flat surface with a definite texture. The air conditioning or heating vents, the floor, the wall, or the bottom of a sports shoe are places to start looking. You'll need a 9 by 12-inch sheet of newsprint and a large dark crayon with the wrapper removed. Place the paper over the texture object and rub gently with the side of the crayon. Make sure you hold the paper securely. If the section you are rubbing is large or the area has a very subtle texture, you may wish to tape your paper in place. After you have finished one rubbing, try doing another one. This time, after you have completed about half of the rubbing, move the paper slightly. Replacing the dark crayon with another color, continue the rubbing. You will get an interesting double image.

PRINCIPLES OF DESIGN

The principles of design are the rules by which an artist uses the elements of design. Although they may vary slightly according to the person using them, the principles most often used in visual art are: *balance, emphasis, movement, variety, proportion, and unity.*

BALANCE

If you dance, ride a bicycle, or play a sport, you know what balance is. Balance is the position of your body so you do not fall. In art, balance is the arrangement of lines, colors, values, textures, forms, and space so that one section or side of the painting does not look heavier or stronger than another.

There are three types of balance: formal or symmetrical, informal or asymmetrical, and radial balance. In formal balance all the parts of a design on one side are relatively equal to those on the other. *The Gulf Stream* could be an example of formal balance because the ship and the waterspout are symmetrically placed and create a triangle with the smack boat. *The Gulf Stream* could also be an example of radial balance. In radial balance, an important part of a design is placed in the center. Other parts of the design radiate or move around it. In *The Gulf Stream* the smack boat is in the center, while the sharks, flying fish, waterspout, and ship move around it in a circular motion.

You can look at the painting as having formal or radial balance. You can also say it has a combination of formal balance and radial balance. What is your opinion?

In informal balance the organization of elements is unequal. For instance, a large shape on one side may be juxtaposed by several small shapes on the other.

Activity 1 - Balance   Choose a geometrical shape. From a 12 x 18-inch colored paper, cut the shape you chose in six different sizes. Place the shapes on a sheet of white or colored paper so that they are divided half on one side and half on the other side of the paper. Step back and see if one side of the layout appears heavier than the other. Try moving the shapes from one side to the other so that you have more on one side than the other, but both sides seem to balance. Now take one small piece and use a crayon to change its color to a bright contrasting color. Start all over with the arrangements. What difference does the bright color make in the number of pieces needed to achieve a balance? How does this bright contrasting color affect the balance of the arrangement?

When you have an arrangement you like that demonstrates balance (symmetrical, asymmetrical, or radial), paste all the pieces down. Label this design by its type of **BALANCE**.

EMPHASIS

An artist may choose to make one part of a design or picture more important than another. This is called "emphasis." For example, an object may be larger or brighter than others. This adds interest or focus to a work. The most important part of Homer's painting, of course, is the man in the boat. Homer emphasized this by making the boat a solid shape and form. It is smooth and white with a brown deck in contrast to the rough texture of the blue-green color of the water. The sunlight shining on the deck also emphasizes it by making it stand out.

Activity 2 - Emphasis   Choose a geometrical shape and cut six copies of it in varying sizes from a 9 x 12-inch sheet of gray or tan paper. Place the shapes in a line on a 12 x 18-inch sheet of paper. Step back and look at the arrangement. Do any of the pieces catch your eye? Do they all look much the same? Select one shape and use a crayon to change the color to a much brighter shade. Replace the piece and again look at the arrangement. Which piece do you see first? Color can be used to achieve emphasis in a work.

Return to the original six neutral shapes. (You'll need to cut out another piece in place of the one you colored.) This time take one of the shapes and add an overall pattern to create a textured surface. You can create your own pattern or do a rubbing to achieve a textured effect. Replace the piece in the pattern and observe. Does texture also contribute to the principle of emphasis? When you have an arrangement that demonstrates emphasis, paste the pieces down. Label the design **EMPHASIS**.

MOVEMENT

The use of lines, colors, values, textures, forms, and space to carry or direct the eye of the viewer from one part of the design or picture to another is called movement. Artists create movement in the way that they use these elements of design. You have already seen how Homer accomplished this in *The Gulf Stream* (see diagram, page 16). Homer also created movement in the water itself. What kind of brushstrokes did he use to accomplish this?

Figure 30. This diagram shows the tonal values in *The Gulf Stream*.

**How is movement suggested
here? Student art.**

Activity 3 - Movement   Select a sheet of 12 x 18-inch
white paper and a colored sheet 9 x 12. Out of either sheet
cut a series of geometrical shapes in graduated sizes as in
Activity 2. Arrange them on the page to create the feeling
of movement. Some possibilities are circular, diagonal,
vertical.

Next, try placing the shapes to create a movement that
goes back into the distance.

Choose one of your arrangements and paste it to the
background. With a marker make a line that shows the
movement. Label the design **MOVEMENT**.

Compare your design with those of classmates. Make a
display of designs in categories. Hang up all arrangements
showing circular movement in one section of the display. Do
the same with other categories. How many different kinds of
movement are in the display?

VARIETY AND CONTRAST

An artist uses the elements of art to create diversity and
differences in a design. Contrasting colors, textures, and
patterns all add interest to a work. Notice how the sharks in
Homer's painting are the same value—dark-gray—as the
water. For contrast, Homer added just a small bit of white to
the tail of the shark in the lower right corner, and painted
dashes of white and red spray where the shark flips its tail.

Activity 4 - Variety and Contrast   Use one 12 x 18-inch sheet of white paper for a background. Choose a light colored piece of 9 x 12-inch paper. Cut the colored paper into a set of a geometrical shapes of the same size. Arrange them so that they have variety of space, movement, and balance. When you're satisfied with your design, paste it on the background paper. Next add variety and contrast. Use felt markers to change the surface appearance of the shapes. You might change the colors or textures of some shapes. Or you could add highlights of color to the corners or edges of some shapes. When complete, label your design **VARIETY AND CONTRAST**.

PROPORTION

The size of one part of an artwork to its other parts is called proportion. Artists use proportion to show emphasis, distance and use of space, and balance. In *The Gulf Stream*, notice the difference in size between the man and the smack boat to the rest of the painting. They are larger than everything except the waves and the large shark in front. The other sharks are about the same size as the man. The man is tall enough to reach from one side of the deck to the other. Are they all in proportion to the story? How important is the size of the ship and the waterspout to the story of the painting? If they were larger they would look closer. If they were smaller, they would be farther away. Does their closeness and size seem right to you? Imagine them smaller and larger. Would that change their relationship to the man in the boat and the total design?

Activity 5 - Proportion   Take two pieces of 12 x 18-inch white, gray, or black paper for a background. From a selection of colored 6 x 9-inch sheets, choose one very bright, intense color and one pale, weak color. Measure the smaller sheets into the proportions shown in the diagram. In each space draw a shape that nearly fills it from edge to edge, or just use the shapes as squares and rectangles.

On the first sheet of 12 x 18-inch paper, put one of the largest bright pieces and one of the shapes of the weaker color.

Problem 1:   Make the large intense colors seem less dominant by the way you arrange the smaller pieces.

Problem 2: Make the design with the weaker color more exciting by the way you arrange the smaller pieces.

You may trade your leftover pieces with other students if you wish. Use felt tip markers. You may also cut the smaller pieces up, but you cannot make the largest piece smaller. When you complete your design, paste all the parts on both sheets and label them **PROPORTION 1** and **PROPORTION 2**.

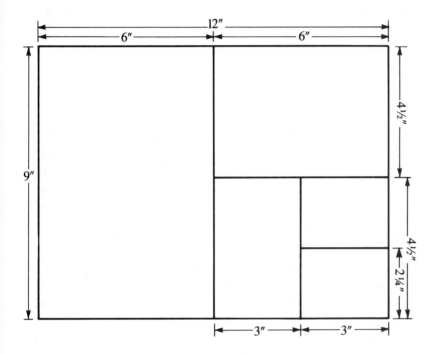

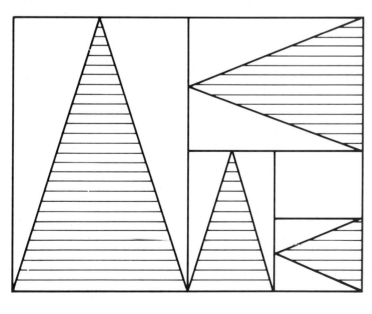

Figure 31. Cut paper to measurements in top diagram. Shaded area indicates geometric cutouts.

UNITY

As you have learned, an artwork has many parts and elements to it. Unity is the result of how all the elements and principles work together. If a work of art has unity, it holds together as a story and as a design. Although a painting may include a ship, a waterspout, a man adrift in a boat, and some sharks, these parts must all have some relation to each other. They must fit together to create the overall message and effect.

Homer achieved unity in several ways. Do you remember how he moved your eye to different parts of *The Gulf Stream* so you would look more closely each time around? In doing that, Homer used composition or the arrangement of parts to give the painting unity. The painting is also unified by the subject matter—the story itself. All the objects, the broken bowsprit and mast, the sharks, the waterspout, the ship, the sugarcane, and the rough sea contribute to the story and mystery surrounding the man in the boat. Homer's main unifying element is color. How does the blue-green water around the boat contribute to the unity of *The Gulf Stream?*

Activity 6 - Unity   Review all the designs you have made. Do they have unity? Do they hold together? If they do not, decide what they need to give them unity. Discuss this with your teacher. Look at the entire series of designs from the activities in this section. Is there unity among them? Do they work as a series showing the principles of design? How do these designs look when you line them up in sequence? Rearrange the sequence to make a better visual arrangement. You now have the contents of a small portfolio on the principles of design. Make a portfolio (**UNITY**) to keep them in.

UNIT

1

CORE ACTIVITIES

MAN versus NATURE:
The Lone Survivor

Winslow Homer's painting, *The Gulf Stream,* portrays a man struggling against the natural forces in the world. Imagine you are a "Lone Survivor" struggling against nature. Select an environment in which you find yourself outdoors (for example, hiking, mountain climbing, swimming, sailing, driving a car in the desert). Then imagine a disaster that occurs to threaten your survival (a hurricane, snowstorm, avalanche, animal, car breakdown). On a sheet of paper divided into six or eight sections, do a sketch of your struggle against nature showing what took place before, during, and after the catastrophe.

After completing the sketch, select the one frame that contains the most action or reveals the most information about the disaster. Using tempera or watercolor, paint an enlarged version of that frame titled **The Lone Survivor**.

MAN IN NATURE:
Globe Spinning

Spin the globe and select an environment in the world—a country, state, or body of water—to research. You can consult magazines, encyclopedias, or other books to find out as much as possible about your chosen location. If, for example,

51

you have chosen a country or a state, find out how the people there work and use the environment to benefit humanity. The purpose of this project is to study people in harmony with the environment. Winslow Homer's man was a sailor who worked the ocean. If you have selected a body of water, you can study the fish which inhabit the water. Or, you could extend the idea of water for beaches and tourism.

Create a collage to reflect people in harmony with the environment you have selected. Your piece should include objects that represent the location and the people in harmony with their surroundings at work and play.

CAMOUFLAGE IN ART:
Hidden Clues

In *The Gulf Stream* Homer used camouflage to fool the viewer concerning the number of sharks in the painting. Camouflage is a technique that many artists use.

Select an animal, bird, or insect in the environment that camouflages itself and design the creature using materials suggested by your teacher. On a separate sheet of paper, create the camouflage environment using the same colors, patterns, line, and texture found in the animal. Then place your creature in or on the drawing so that the camouflage is apparent to a viewer.

MAN IN ACTION:
Body Language

Look at the positioning of the man in the boat in *The Gulf Stream*. How did Homer use perspective to create a tension between the body and the environment. As you create your own action forms discuss your use of motion and proportion.

REARRANGE THE MASTERPIECE:
Seascapes

Homer selected specific objects, color, lighting, and placements to achieve a certain effect in *The Gulf Stream*.

Would Homer's painting be any different if the objects in the painting were located elsewhere on the canvas? Would the painting have the same message if the objects appeared in different places?

Make a separate painting or drawing of all of the following objects from *The Gulf Stream:*

waves	ship	sharks	waterspout
boat	man	flying fish	

Then cut out each object and rearrange them on another piece of paper which has the sky and water drawn on it. For example, place the sharks in the background, the ship in the foreground, and so forth.

Then compare your rearranged *The Gulf Stream* to Homer's. Does your work suggest humor instead of terror? Does your painting have the same or different message?

THE ARTIST
SPEAKS
ABOUT NATURE

You have learned how important nature was to the work of the painter Winslow Homer. In the unit that follows you will see how many other artists have used the natural environment for their inspiration, too. First, let's "listen" to five artists speaking about what they see in nature.

Joseph Mallord William Turner (British, 1775-1851)

"I paint what I see, not what I know."

Study Turner's seascape, *Snowstorm: Steamboat Off Harbor's Mouth*. What is the artist showing us? Did Turner ever really see such a sight on the ocean? When Turner speaks of seeing, he means more than just seeing with our eyes. He wants the viewer to feel the drama of the scene as well. To show this in his painting, he used dazzling light, color, and motion. He gives us only an impression of a ship with a dark hull and a flag flying bravely from the mast. He uses fantastic colors and the sun's reflection to contrast with the helpless ship.

During storms at sea, Turner had sailors tie him to the mast so that he could study the effects of wind and rain on the water. What Turner saw was how weak people are before the destructive power of nature.

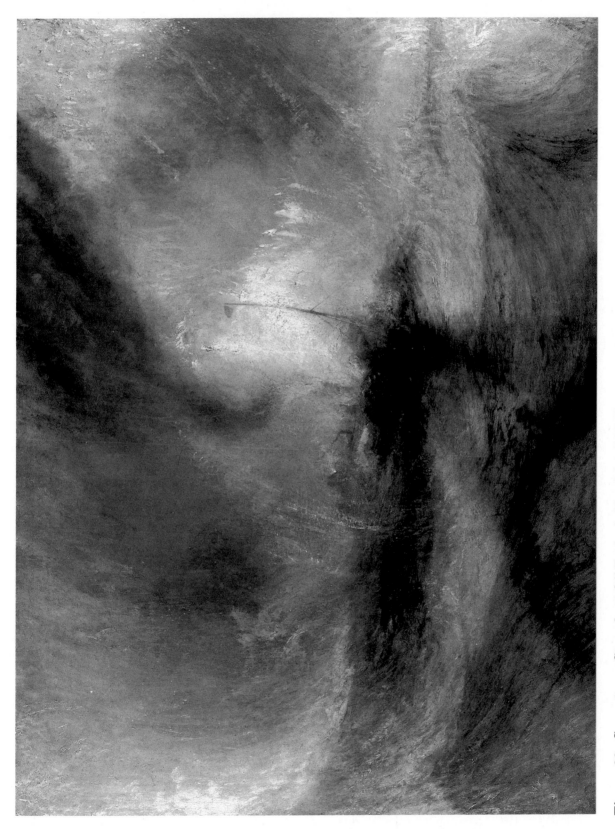

Figure 32. *Snowstorm: Steamboat Off Harbor's Mouth* by J.M.W. Turner depicts the awesome forces of nature. (1842)

Vincent Van Gogh (Dutch, 1853-1890)

Vincent Van Gogh wrote in a letter to his brother Theo in 1888: "Colors give me extraordinary feelings.... I shall do another picture this very night.... When nature is so beautiful, I am not aware of myself anymore and the pictures come to me as in a dream."

Look at the painting *The Starry Night*. What feelings do you think Van Gogh had when he painted it? What kind of a dream do you think Van Gogh was in when this picture came to him?

Figure 33. Vincent Van Gogh created a dream world in his painting *The Starry Night* completed in 1889.

Figure 34. In *The Stampede*, Frederic Remington shows riders racing before the violence of nature.

Frederic Remington (American, 1861-1909)

"I think man was never called on to do a more desperate deed than running in the night with longhorns taking the country as it comes and with the cattle splitting out behind him, all as mad as thunder and lightning above him; while the cut banks and prairie dog holes wail below. Nature is merciless!"

Remington's painting is called *The Stampede*. What does that tell you about how he saw nature? Remington's painting is called a narrative painting because it tells a story. Study the painting. What is the story it tells? How do Remington's words help you understand it?

Piet Mondrian (Dutch, 1872-1944)

"Every artist has always been moved by beauty of line, colour, and relationship for their own sake and not by what they may represent."

Between 1909 and 1912, Piet Mondrian made three paintings of a tree, in three different styles. The paintings are called *The Red Tree, The Grey Tree,* and *The Flowering Apple Tree.* After looking at the paintings, read Mondrian's explanation again. What does a tree mean to Mondrian?

Figure 35. In *The Red Tree* by Piet Mondrian, the tree's form is still easily identifiable.

Figure 36. Mondrian's *The Grey Tree* has more lines and less leaves.

Figure 37. Mondrian's *The Flowering Apple Tree* is a series of lines suggested by the shape of a tree.

Figure 35.

Figure 36.

Figure 37.

Claude Oscar Monet (French, 1840—1926)

"Monet only has an eye, but what an eye!"

And what a statement by Paul Cézanne about his fellow artist Claude Oscar Monet! Look at Monet's *Haystack at Sunset*. What did the master impressionist see?

In front is a large stack. On the top, dark purple tones are set off against a color opposite—the yellows of the sky. An orange-red sunset reflects glorious color on the ground hitting the tomato-red bottom of the stack. The choppy brushstrokes create rhythms of a ballet—where the grass sways and the stack shimmers.

But "Monet's eye" saw more. Around 1890 he did a series of stacks at different times of day and seasons of the year. "The title *Haystack* is wrong. They are wheat stacks," said Monet. And he knew the difference since he had grown up in farm country. Wheat stacks are tied and thatched to keep the rain out. Wheat is the wealth of the farmer and he watches over it like his own house. Notice how the stack carefully repeats the shape of the houses in back. This stack is so powerful it beams an image of a dwelling and Monet's poetic statement reminds us of the human bond with life-giving nature.

Figure 38. Monet's eye not only saw nature, but experienced it as well. (1891)

UNIT 2

FORMS OF EXPRESSION

The Artist and Nature

THE ARTIST'S VISION

This book is about the visual arts. The visual arts represent various ways of seeing; that is, what the artist sees, and what the viewer sees. Talking about what we see and why we see it helps us to discover explanations for things. Such discoveries are called interpretations, and each of us may have a different interpretation for the same work of art.

The French painter Henri Matisse has this to say about seeing: "The artist has to look at everything as though he saw it for the first time: he has to look at life as he did when he was a child and, if he loses that faculty, he cannot express himself in an original, that is, a personal way."

Another painter, an American named Charles Burchfield, recalls: "I saw a sketch this evening that gave me the same savage thrill that I felt when as a boy I sighted a new butterfly or moth."

LOOKING AT NATURE
THROUGH PAINTINGS

Nature offers the artist a wide range of possibilities for expression. Marc Chagall said: "Art picks up where nature ends." He meant that the artist's vision gives us a new look at nature. The artist can celebrate nature, record it exactly, or distort it to show that nature is ideal, romantic, comforting, frightening, or fantastic. The artist can, through images, attempt to control nature or show the relationships between people and nature.

You have spent some time reading about and looking at Winslow Homer's painting *The Gulf Stream.* Homer knew a lot about nature when he painted this picture. Let's turn now to the works of other painters to see how they open our eyes to nature.

Sidney Goodman, an American artist from Philadelphia, painted a picture called *Landscape with Four Towers.* A landscape shows a view of the scenery on the land. Goodman's painting reflects his concern about the changes people cause in landscapes. "*Landscape with Four Towers* was not any specific locale," Goodman says. "It is a composite

Figure 39. *Landscape with Four Towers* **expresses Sidney Goodman's feelings about the way people alter the natural landscape.**

growing out of observation of the landscape approaching New York City on the New Jersey Turnpike....I have been interested in the way manmade structures too often violate a place or the landscape. I both recoil at this intrusion, and find myself drawn to it."

Look carefully at *Landscape with Four Towers*. What do you see in this painting? There are four passages from bottom to top in the landscape. The bottom third shows ravaged hillsides with a sprinkling of surviving trees. Just above is a community of farms and houses, appearing cozy and peaceful. Above and beyond this section is a gray, cold-looking section of what appear to be industrial plants and office buildings. At the top, weighing down the other three sections like massive paperweights, are the four towers. Why do they sit poised and waiting over the city and the land? Why do they look so threatening? Even the artist said he felt he was witnessing something horrible.

The four towers look as if they are perched on the edge of the world. Perhaps the artist meant to show they are on the edge of modern history. Notice that there is light falling on one side of the towers and darkness on the other. Was the artist thinking of good versus evil? Here, then, is a landscape with four different stories, showing an aspect of people and nature at each level. As our eye is led up and out of the painting by the bright sky and pointing towers, the artist might be asking us to provide the fifth story. What do you think it might be?

We are discovering that artists see and record their responses to nature in many different ways. Let us look at another example.

Close your eyes and imagine a starry night. What do the night stars look like in your mind's eye? Now look again at the painting, *The Starry Night*, by the Dutch painter Vincent Van Gogh. Have you ever seen a starry night like that? How is it different from the one you saw when you closed your eyes?

Does this landscape in Van Gogh's painting look real? To Van Gogh it did. He had a great imagination and a very individual view of reality. The hills in this painting swell like ocean waves. The stars whirl and explode. A huge poplar tree weaves and points to the heavens. Yet while the night leaps like flames from the canvas, the little town and its church sleep quietly. Van Gogh painted his visions in an unforgettable way.

Figure 40. In *The Starry Night*, Vincent Van Gogh portrayed the world in a new and imaginative way.

Look again at *The Starry Night*. How does Van Gogh create such a powerful landscape? The village appears distant because of the dark colors and the gentle brushstrokes. The dark tree pulls your eye to the sky, and there the bright color and the stabbing brushstrokes almost envelop you. If your eye escapes for a moment back to the village, it is swept by the weaving tree into the whirling sky again. So you are twirled around and around in this painting. It is a disquieting picture.

To add to the sense of vibration, Van Gogh has used mostly blue, violet, and yellow. Violet and yellow are complementary colors which, when used like this, tend to create a sense of excitement in the eyes of the viewer.

Artists use many different ways to make a landscape interesting to the viewer. In *The Starry Night*, the whirling stars almost suck us into the picture. Through intense color, strong brushstrokes, and powerful rhythms, the artist has communicated to us an amazing landscape.

What ways can *you* think of to attract the attention of a viewer? How would you get a viewer into your landscape?

Look now at the painting called *Travelers in Autumn Mountains*. This ink painting on silk was done about A.D.1350 by the Chinese artist Sheng Mou. It makes a strong statement about the relationship of people and nature. In the painting travelers move unhurriedly along a gentle road. We join the travelers on the road, but at the same time we have an overview of the entire landscape.

Figure 41. *Travelers in Autumn Mountains* by Sheng Mou. The tiny figures are overwhelmed by the grandeur of nature.

Nature looms and stretches before our eyes in this beautiful painting. We are encouraged by the breathtaking mountains, the lovely waterfall, the pleasant trees, and interesting curves in the hills. We move about the landscape slowly and think about what we are seeing. Sheng Mou is telling us that mankind is not the most important element in the scheme of things, but merely a traveler passing through the universe.

Early Chinese landscapes, such as *Travelers in Autumn Mountains* or *Landscape with Snow* (page 67), do not tell us where the viewer stands in relation to the view shown. The Chinese artist assumes that we are in the landscape, not looking at it from the outside.

We might find it difficult to believe that the fantastic mountain peaks we are looking at could represent a real landscape. Yet such scenery is actually to be found in parts of China. The artist brings it to our attention by painting a landscape both of boundless views and close, detailed description.

When you look at *Travelers in Autumn Mountains*, what do you see first? Mountains? Trees? Waterfall? Travelers? Everything at once? In this painting the human figures are as much a part of nature as the trees or the mountains.

What does *Travelers in Autumn Mountains* have in common with Van Gogh's *The Starry Night*? The first is a gentle but powerful landscape; the second is an exciting and powerful landscape. Both portray mankind as just part of a larger natural force. Both say some similar things in different ways.

If you could see the original paintings of these two works, you would discover yet another interesting similarity between them. The brushstroke is very important in creating the "look" of both paintings. We find gentleness and calm in *Travelers in Autumn Mountains* and anxiety and movement in *The Starry Night*. Although paintings are often thought of as two-dimensional compared to sculpture, which is three-dimensional, they are in fact not flat. The paint or ink is applied, usually with a brush, on a support ground such as paper or canvas or wood. The impression left on the ground by the stroke of the brush is like the artist's handwriting or imprint. When we visit an art museum we can look closely at original paintings and study the brushstrokes. They help us to better understand the artist's intentions.

Figure 42. The figures in a Chinese painting *Landscape with Snow*, of the 13th century, are humbled by nature as were the figures in Sheng Mou's painting.

The brushstroke is very important in Chinese and Japanese painting. The stroke itself can be carefully controlled or bold and free. It must express the spirit of the artist as well as an awareness of the life of nature.

Artists of the Orient have a remarkable way of expressing the forms of living nature through the energy and discipline of the brushstroke.

The technique of the Chinese landscape painter has four basic elements: the line, the ink wash, the texture stroke, and the dot. The last two are used to give texture and accent to rocks and mountains. Can you find examples of all four of these elements in Sheng Mou's painting? Vincent Van Gogh admired Japanese art. Do you think this might have influenced his use of broken lines and strong texture strokes in *The Starry Night*?

Chinese and Japanese painters traditionally copy the work of the old masters, carefully studying their brushwork. In this way they train their hands while learning both the techniques of painting and respect for the tradition.

Figure 43 shows two paintings by the same artist, Tao-Chi (Chinese, 1642–1707). One is in the style of another artist, Ni Tsan, the other is an original. Look carefully at both of them. Can you tell which has the copied style and which was in Tao Chi's own style? In the copy the lines and brushstrokes are stiff and heavy, but in the original they are free and alive.

The copy is the painting on the left. Even though the subject matter is different, look at the way the bamboo in each picture is painted. In the original the brushstroke is more natural and relaxed. The lines for the pumpkin and squash are free and have feeling to them. In the copy, the brushstrokes are stiff, and in some places painted over. They lack the directness of the artist. The copy does not express as well as the original the aliveness of nature.

Artists have used several ways of learning from each other. Some are inspired by the ideas of other artists and borrow only what is of particular interest to them. A marriage of two different ideas or styles can produce a new, fresh way of expression. The visual arts are filled with examples of such marriages.

Figure 43. Oriental ink paintings by Tao-Chi
(1642–1707). (a) *Landscape in Style of Ni Tsan*
(dated 1697), (b) *Bamboo, Vegetables, and Fruit*
(dated 1705).

In this early Chinese painting (Figure 44), you get the feeling of the artist's poem, which says, "When there is nothing to do, this is a peaceful place to live, and the mountains are beautiful."

Two more paintings show how artists see people in nature. *Hunters in the Snow* is by the Flemish painter Pieter Brueghel the Elder. Flemish people live in a part of northern Europe called Flanders. Most of Flanders lies in the countries of Belgium and France. *View of Toledo* is by a painter known as El Greco "The Greek", who although born in Crete, did most of his work in Spain in the late 1500's. In what ways are *Hunters in the Snow* and *Travelers in Autumn Mountains* alike? In what ways are *View of Toledo* and *The Starry Night* alike?

Figure 44. Notice that the Chinese artists often wrote poems on their paintings.

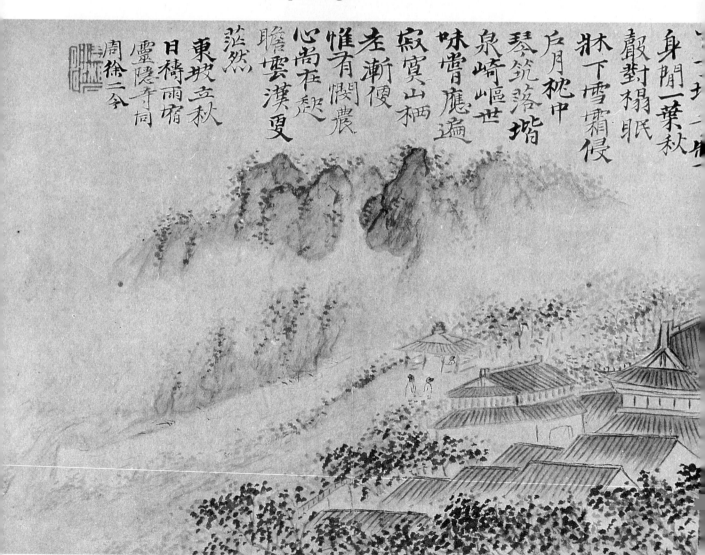

Figure 45. Pieter Brueghel, the Elder, showed the life and landscape of sixteenth-century Flanders in *Hunters in the Snow*. (1565)

Figure 46. El Greco's highly imaginative *View of Toledo* was probably painted between 1595 and 1600.

In all four of these paintings nature is more than a setting for human activities; it is the main subject of the picture. The people and buildings in these works are not as important as the cosmos. All the paintings provide a view that almost takes our breath away. All demonstrate the power of nature.

Many artists have looked at nature in terms of the seasons. *Hunters in the Snow* shows the seasonal work of Flemish people in the 1500s when Brueghel lived. Let's look at three other paintings showing winter in more recent times.

Backyards, Greenwich Village is by the American artist John Sloan. Here is a city landscape where we would least expect to find it—in a small backyard. The backyard has been changed for the moment into a wonderland for children and cats. Even the laundry seems to be flapping happily in the wind and sunshine.

John Sloan was a newspaper staff artist who reported the passing scene in illustrations for magazines and newspapers. He knew and loved the life of the city. His pictures show a warm caring for people and often a good sense of humor.

Figure 47. John Sloan presents an intimate view of modern city life, in *Backyards, Greenwich Village*, painted in 1914.

Look at the expression on the cat curled up in the fore-ground. How does the little girl who is watching feel? Sloan seems to be saying that we don't need the big countryside when it snows; there is much pleasure to be found even in a little box of a yard.

February by John Twachtman has caught the wonder of winter in the New England woods. Twachtman, another American artist, also studied Japanese prints. Like the Far Eastern landscape painters, he tried to capture in his work the true spirit of nature. Twachtman spent his life painting only landscapes.

February is a quiet, peaceful landscape. It is not filled with people and winter activities as are *Hunters in the Snow*

Figure 48. *February* **by John Henry Twachtman depicts a world undisturbed by human activity.**

and *Backyards, Greenwich Village*. There is not even a solitary traveler to walk through this winter day with us. Instead we are alone with the snowy hills, the frozen stream, a few trees, and our thoughts. Everything in the painting is of equal value; it is as though we are looking through a veil. There is nothing to distract us. Nothing grabs at us. Nothing pulls us into the picture. We simply look in wonder at the beauty of a landscape transformed by snow.

Twachtman wrote: "I can see how necessary it is to live always in the country—at all seasons of the year. We must have snow and lots of it. Never is nature more lovely than when it is snowing. Everything is so quiet and the whole earth seems wrapped in a mantle...all nature is hushed to silence."

The Wreck of the Hoffnung by the German artist Caspar David Friedrich is also known as *The Polar Sea*. *The Polar Sea* does not invite us to play, nor does it charm us with its beauty. It shows us another side of snow and ice. It tells us to stay away by showing how nature can defeat us. There is nothing here to soften the effect. The ice slabs almost cut us even as we look upon them.

Figure 49. *The Polar Sea,* **by Caspar David Friedrich depicts human effort defeated by nature. (1824)**

This painting was inspired by a dangerous incident in the Arctic expedition of William Perry in 1819-1820. However, for the artist, the painting is more than a record of an incident. It is a symbol of a defeat by nature. The boat is almost swallowed up by the ice. Its remains are just another broken slab. The ice appears to be like concrete, heavily crushing the ship along with the explorer's hopes and dreams.

Still other painters have shown how people live in harmony with nature. Look now at the watercolor painting called *Indians Fishing* by John White. This is a picture filled with life: plants, fish, birds, and American Indians. The light in this painting is soft and gentle. The Indians have pleasant expressions on their faces. People and nature are at peace.

Figure 50. John White's early American painting, *Indians Fishing*, is a vision of harmony between people and the land they inhabit. (1585)

Figure 51. *The Great Wave Off Kanagawa* **by Hokusai.**

White's watercolor, *Indians Fishing,* may be the first landscape painting of America. English ships voyaging to the New World in the late 16th century sometimes took along an artist in order to bring back descriptions of the life they might find there. John White arrived off the Carolina banks in 1585 and became the first artist to make drawings of the Indians, animals, and plants in the region.

The seas have provided artists with a sometimes spectacular form of nature—the wave. Let's look at two works of art using waves as a central focus. In both, fingerlike projections of white foam reach out. You are already familiar with *The Great Wave Off Kanagawa,* by thc Japanese artist Hokusai. The wave in this picture rises from the sea. Its huge, dark form is lifted by frothy fingers of foam feeling for the little men in their boats. So large is the wave, that even Mount Fuji is dwarfed. *The Great Wave Off Kanagawa* suggests tremendous weight and sheer physical power.

The other painting, *Waves* by Ogata Korin, is more mysterious than *The Great Wave Off Kanagawa*. It is filled with lovely, flowing shapes that look something like ghosts. Nature, in the form of these waves, appears to be alive. Can you see eyes looking out at you? *Waves* is a painting one can look at for a long time and discover many surprises. Its power lies in its ability to hold our attention, as well as its rhythms.

Another painter who was fascinated by water was the American Marsden Hartley. He loved waterfalls. In 1937 he painted *Smelt Brook Falls*. He said then: "I have hopes at one time or another to have a show of nothing but waterfalls, as I love them so much."

Figure 52. In *Waves* by Ogata Korin, the huge waves rise up to haunt the viewer. (before 1716)

Figure 53. Violent and peaceful elements coexist in Marsden Hartley's *Smelt Brook Falls* (1937).

Hartley spent ten years wandering about Europe seeking inspiration. It wasn't until his return to America that he found his own strong expression in painting the scenery of the New England coast. He loved the strength and intensity of nature: the churning seas, the deep, jagged woods, the huge rocks and boulders, the icy waters, the pounding wind. It seems fitting that to record his response to such strong and often violent aspects of nature, he worked with rich emotional colors.

Hartley's vision is so strong that he does not need to paint a vast landscape to express his response to nature. A single detail in the landscape will, in his hands, tell the story. *Smelt Brook Falls* tumbles with great force and energy over monumental boulders. We can almost hear the thundering sounds. Even the trees seem excited by this event. They tilt and rock slightly as if to mark the vibrations of the land itself. To strengthen the impact of the scene, Hartley has overemphasized the trees, rocks, and water.

However, at the bottom of the picture we find a quiet pool of water. It is perhaps like the calm that follows a violent storm. In this way, the artist reassures us of the balance of nature.

Animals are very important in many artists' paintings of nature. Look at *Blue Roller* (or *Hooded Crow*) by the German artist Albrecht Dürer. For Dürer the object of interest is the bird itself. He has included every detail he can observe.

Dürer's crow, although dead, draws our attention because it is painted with such precision and gorgeous color. Dürer said he used the "most beautiful" colors he could get, especially the blues, the ultramarines. This blue roller will never fly again, but our eyes are drawn to its wings hanging heavily at its sides. For a moment we see the bird in flight. What special skill it takes to show us a dead bird and make us think about flight!

Figure 54. *Sea Crab* (1495) is another example of Dürer's desire to render faithfully the natural world.

Figure 55. *Blue Roller* (1512)
shows Albrecht Dürer's
great powers of observation.

In Dürer's *Sea Crab*, the crab seems to look straight out at us and even beckons us with its front claws to come toward it. Every detail is presented in the most delicate colors. *Sea Crab* is, however, more than an observation of nature; it is a portrait. What a character we are looking at! Could the crab be thinking the same thing as it looks at us?

Dürer worked with great concentration on only one thing at a time. He had learned a thorough sense of craftsmanship from his father, who was a goldsmith. Dürer approached nature with great respect. In fact, perhaps no other artist of his day (1471-1528) recorded nature with such understanding.

LOOKING AT NATURE
THROUGH SCULPTURE

You have learned how nature has affected the work of many different painters. You have also seen how artists use nature, or some part of it, to express their visions. Many artists express themselves in other media. Some work in wood, clay, stone, or other materials. These artists carve, mold, weld, and sometimes hammer. These artist are sculptors.

Like painters, sculptors are also affected by nature. They, too, have a vision to share.

The sculptress, Barbara Hepworth, remembers how deeply affected she was, during drives with her father, by the countryside of Yorkshire, in England, where she was born: "And the country—the unspoiled country there—was so magnificently shaped that the roads became, as it were, contours over a sculpture."

Ideas that began to form in her mind during those childhood trips, Hepworth claims, shaped her whole life. "The hills were sculptures; the roads defined the form. Above all, there was the sensation of moving physically over the contours of fullnesses and concavities, through hollows and over peaks—feeling, touching, seeing, through mind and hand and eye. This sensation has never left me. I, the sculptor, am the landscape. I am the form and I am the hollow, the thrust and the contour."

Look at Hepworth's *Figure in a Landscape*. What do you see? Where is the figure? Where, for that matter, is the landscape? Hepworth says, "I, the sculptor, am the landscape." In this work could the two holes be her own eyes? Could the form itself represent a mask through which she views nature? Such forms are called "pure" forms. They do not imitate a mountain or a wave or a sea form. Still, in Hepworth's work, there is a power in the form that makes us look longer at it and wonder if it has some special meaning. As Matisse advised us, it takes an effort to see.

Hepworth called her sculpture *Figure in a Landscape*. The name demands that we make the effort to see what she had in mind when she carved it. The sculpture itself appears to be looking at us to capture our attention.

Barbara Hepworth was impressed early in her life that a dirty industrial town such as Wakefield, her hometown, could grow out of the beautiful countryside surrounding it. To Hepworth, this seemed a conflict between people and nature. Yet she also saw that the town and countryside were part of the same landscape, and this suggested to her a unity between people and nature. Hepworth's sculpture represents her efforts at expressing both this conflict and unity.

Why did Barbara Hepworth choose to work in stone? She tells us in her own words:

"I so love carving. It seems to me the most rhythmical and marvelous way of working on live and sensuous material because, even if one has two pieces of the same stone, they have another nature. Every piece of wood and every piece of stone has its own particular live quality of growth, crystal structure, and one becomes utterly absorbed ... as one tries to make the forms and contours which will express oneself....Being a carver, I do have a complete conception in my mind of the form I'm making before I start carving or, indeed, making any work."

Figure 56. British sculptress Barbara Hepworth translated her sensations of traveling over the land in her *Figure in a Landscape*.

Recall for a moment the German artist Albrecht Dürer, who painted *Blue Roller* and *Sea Crab*. Dürer recorded nature with great care, yet his works had a life far beyond their precise details. Dürer once said, "For in truth art is implicit in nature, and whoever can extract it has it." Dürer lived and worked in the 15th and 16th centuries. Yet for many centuries before Dürer's time, artists were extracting art from nature. Let us look at three sculptures that were produced in China thousands of years ago.

The very earliest sculptures found in China include a jade "bird." This sculpture was made during the Neolithic period (or Stone Age), which lasted from about 3000 to about 1600 B.C. Pottery of the Neolithic period decorated with plant forms, birds, animals, and human figures has also been found in China.

Do you think this figure is a bird? If not, what might it be? What is it doing? The "bird" appears to be resting but, at the same time, alert. Its neck thrusts upward, suggesting the "bird" is aware and prepared to fly if necessary. The artist must have been very observant to create a feeling of both rest and alertness in one figure.

Now look at the marble sculpture of the powerful sitting bear. It was carved during the Shang dynasty in China (about 1600-1027 B.C.). Carvings and paintings of such

Figure 57. The abstract bird carved in jade is among the earliest known sculptures from China, circa 1500 B.C.

Figure 58. The sitting bear
carved in marble is another
fine example of very early
Chinese sculpture.

animals have been found in tombs of the Shang kings. These
animals were there partly to protect the tombs. They were
also there for their decorative value. In other words, their
shapes and designs were pleasurable just to look at.

The bear is decorative—striking and attractive—and we
can enjoy looking at it simply as an ornament. However,
look at the bear more closely. Does it appear to be pro-
tective? Is it ferocious? Calm? Or is it proud and self-
confident as a creature might be that is aware of its strength
and power? This bear holds itself almost like a little king.
With its feet planted squarely on the ground and its head
and chest raised, it seems to be saying, "I am a bear to
reckon with!" Perhaps, then, the bear is protecting the spirit
of the dead king. As in the case of the "bird," the artist
displays in the sculpture of the bear careful thought and
observation.

Finally, look at the small bird carved in jade. It was meant to be a pendant, worn on a chain around someone's neck. This bird was made sometime between 1027 and 249 B.C. The simple design expresses motion.

Now compare the early Chinese bird sculptures—the Neolithic "bird" and the bird pendant—to another sculpture, *Bird in Space*. *Bird in Space* was created in 1925 by the Romanian sculptor Constantin Brancusi. All three sculptures are abstractions. This means that their forms represent or recall an idea or concept, but they do not show it just as our eye usually sees it. For instance, the form of the Neolithic "bird" merely suggests a bird; it does not show an exact bird.

The other two sculptures suggest a movement we associate with birds—flight. The outstretched wings of the bird pendant tell us that it is flying. How does the Brancusi sculpture suggest flight? What is the form doing? Does it look as if it is standing still or as if it is moving? In what direction is it moving?

Brancusi wanted to remove as many details as possible from a bird and still give us a sense of flying. He said, "All my life I have sought the essence of flight. Don't look for mysteries. I give you pure joy. Look at the sculptures until you see them." Well, then, let's look at *Bird in Space* until we see it. What details has Brancusi completely eliminated from the bird? What is still birdlike about the form?

Brancusi explored bird forms in many sculptures, until he finally saw the image of the bird as just the *idea* of flight. In fact, he repeated the theme of *Bird in Space* between the years 1924 and 1949 in a series of works that were increasingly simplified.

He was always looking for basic forms that appear over and over again in nature. A basic shape is one that cannot be simplified any further. One of Brancusi's favorite basic shapes was the oval. In nature we find it as an embryo, a nucleus, and an egg, for example. What do all three have in common? They are all beginnings of life.

Brancusi used the basic oval shape for beginnings too— beginnings of sculptures. Look again at the sculpture *Bird in Space* and then at Brancusi's sculpture *Fish*. Both are basically an oval shape. *Bird in Space* is an oval that has been stretched upward as if soaring into the sky. It is an oval that stands for flight. Because it has no special details, it is not one particular bird but all birds—and all flight. *Fish* is an oval that has been flattened and stretched out horizon-

Figure 59.

Figure 61.

Figure 59. The simple design of this small jade bird expresses the feeling of flight.

Figure 60. *Fish* carved in 1930 by Constantin Brancusi.

Figure 61. The modern sculptor Constantin Brancusi expresses the essence of flight in *Bird in Space*. (1925)

Figure 60.

tally. It hovers motionlessly the way fish do when they are still. However, like the Neolithic "bird," it looks ready to dart away in a moment.

Since Brancusi's sculptures were so stark and simple in form, he cared a great deal about their finish. The artist polished and repolished their surfaces and contours until they seemed to glow with the ideas they contained within.

LOOKING AT NATURE THROUGH PHOTOGRAPHY

Still another form in which artists explore nature is the photograph. In this medium the artist works with images on film. Like other artists, the photographer must have a vision, and must find a way to express it through the lens of a camera focused on the outside world.

Robert Frank's photograph *Santa Fe, New Mexico* is one of many from his book *The Americans*. Frank traveled throughout America photographing the commonplace. He wanted to show us the American landscape as he saw it, filled with plain people in a plain landscape, going about their business. He wanted to make us notice places and events we might tend to overlook. He wanted to make us see new meanings in everyday events.

Santa Fe, New Mexico can be seen as a powerful comment on people and nature. Five little gas pumps stand on a landscape. They might have arrived moments ago from outer space. They stand at attention, their little round heads all turned in the same direction, as if awaiting a command; their hoses ready at their sides. Where did they come from? What are they doing?

The gas pumps, of course, were made by people to serve people with a product taken from the land. In a way, they are indeed invaders. For centuries before their arrival, nothing disturbed the flat stretches of land. Only a few junipers and pinon trees punctuated the landscape.

Why did the photographer make the sign, SAVE, such an important part of the picture? What did it actually mean? Probably that gas was sold for less at that station. What did the photographer want the viewer to think about? To save the landscape from such intruders? To save us all from too much progress? The photograph *Santa Fe, New Mexico* appears to be straightforward. Yet we might say there is more to it than meets the eye. It is a powerful photograph

Figure 62. *Santa Fe, New Mexico,* **a photograph of commonplace objects by Robert Frank, gives a thought-provoking image.**

that sneaks up on us. Like Barbara Hepworth's sculpture, it looks back at us, holding our attention, forcing us to think about it.

Two additional photographs show how other artists saw manmade forms interrupting the natural landscape. One is Charles Sheeler's *Fuel Tanks, Wisconsin.* The other photograph is Barry Brukoff's *Stonehenge.*

Sometimes a work of art appears to be almost an exact copy of nature. If so, we say, "Why, that is just like a photograph!" However, we would not be talking about a photograph such as the one called *Boojum II* by Richard Misrach. Look closely at this photograph. What is it about?

Figure 63. Charles Sheeler's *Fuel Tanks, Wisconsin* shows how manufactured objects can dominate a landscape.

Figure 64. *Stonehenge* by Barry Brukoff focuses on the weighty presence of this ancient subject. (© *1980 Barry Brukoff*)

Figure 65. Richard Misrach produced an eerie landscape in his photograph *Boojum II*. (1977)

Boojum II was created through dramatic lighting and special techniques in the darkroom. The end product is a highly subjective, or personal, view of the subject. *Boojum II* almost shocks us into seeing in this landscape something that Misrach did. The trees seem to be thrusting from the earth, reaching out with clawlike limbs. Where are they coming from? What time of day is it? The black edge around the photograph makes it look like a frame from a movie.

What do you think this photograph is about? Is it an exciting or a frightening picture? What does the title, *Bojum II* suggest about this landscape?

Compare *Boojum II* to the photograph *Leafless Oak Tree* by William Henry Fox Talbot. *Leafless Oak Tree* is a more traditional photograph. It was made in the mid-nineteenth century and looks exactly like what it is—an oak tree. Which photograph is more interesting? Which do you prefer? Why?

Figure 66. William Henry Fox Talbot's *Leafless Oak Tree* **shows a natural object as it really appears. (1840)**

THE CAMERA RECORDS NATURE

Photography was invented in the early part of the nineteenth century. Painters as well as the general public admired the camera's ability to record nature in exact detail. However, most people regarded photography as the work of a machine and not as an art form.

Since most early photographers were interested in commercial or scientific success, they did not even consider the problem. The miracle of a life-like image was more than enough.

Only gradually did the camera record the vision of the human being behind it. In the next three photographs, we will look at the works of two early American masters— Edward Steichen (1879–1973), Edward Weston (1886–1958)—and the British photographer, E. James Muybridge (1830–1904). The ways their cameras recorded nature transformed photography into an art form. The public could

Figure 67. *Landscape-Moonlight* (1904) **by Edward Steichen.**

now see and understand the mastery of the photographer-artist over the "machine."

Edward Steichen

Edward Steichen photographed *Landscape - Moonlight* in 1904. It is one of the most beautiful and important photographs ever made. It has the feel of a painting. The mist has a haunting and dramatic effect. The eerie moon creates a moody atmosphere over the long shadows of the trees in the water. Steichen was a leader in the movement away from the camera's simple ability to copy nature. He was a painter with a keen interest in making artistic photographs.

Around 1904 he did an art series that expressed the mysterious atmosphere of moonlit landscapes. Steichen also experimented with exposure times in photographic printing. Sometimes accidents happened: When his camera lens got wet from a downpour, the image shot was blurred—with great effect!

Edward Weston

Edward Weston began his career by doing artistic photographs called *pictorialism*. He then developed camera techniques and photographs with absolute sharpness. Weston looked for the "grand design" of the universe, and his photographs reveal many abstract patterns in nature. Weston felt it necessary for the photographer to see clearly in the mind's eye the final result of the shot—before shooting the photograph—including the lights and darks. The print could not be changed! Now look at the cool design of nature in *Iceberg Lake*. You are experiencing this abstract wonderland through the lens of a modern artist.

Figure 68. *Iceberg Lake* **(1937) by Edward Weston.**

Figure 69. *Mirror Lake—Valley of the Yosemite*, **by the British photographer E. James Muybridge.**

E. James Muybridge

E. James Muybridge worked in Britain and the United States. He was a brilliant artist and quite inventive. His incredible shot, *Mirror Lake—Valley of the Yosemite*, was made over a hundred years ago. The double image of Muybridge's camera is a perfect description of the lake's name—Mirror Lake. But where did Muybridge stand when he took this photograph? How was he able to record that kind of reflection? Note the trees in the background are also reflected in the water. This is a marvelous composition created by an ingenious photographer.

LOOKING AT NATURE
THROUGH ARCHITECTURE

Earlier in this unit you read that things that are very different can be related. How different a painting is from a building, and yet these works of art, too, can be related.

Look at the Sydney Opera House in the illustration. A Danish architect, Jorn Utzon, won first prize in a competition for designing this building in 1956. His design was thought to be daring, dramatic, and original. It consists of huge shells over the opera house. It is a very modern-looking and dazzling building. Look again at the paintings *The Great Wave Off Kanagawa* and *Waves* on pps. 77–78. Do you find any similarities in the forms represented in those paintings and those in the opera house? It is known that Utzon, the architect, was influenced by Japanese culture.

Figure 70. The Opera House in Sydney, Australia, was designed by Jorn Utzon in 1956.

Figure 71. "Falling water," designed by Frank Lloyd Wright, blends perfectly with its natural setting. (1937)

The house called "Falling water" was designed by another architect who admired Japanese culture and the Japanese respect for nature. Frank Lloyd Wright (1867-1959) grew up in Wisconsin, in a small town in a countryside filled with meadows, cliffs, and wooded hills. As a young boy he found time between farm chores and school to play at designing buildings. Later in his life he asked his wife: "Can you see me there...a curly-headed boy, all alone, sculpting, playing in the sand, constructing a building with branches and rocks, then planting grass around it, making a little garden of flowers—can you see me there?"

Frank Lloyd Wright was interested in the integration of people and nature. He felt that a home should blend with its surroundings so that the atmosphere, the light, and the view all worked with the building. Wright believed that a house is a place where people live, not just where they sleep. In order to live, people must have a sense of privacy and a feeling that nature is alive around them.

Falling water blends with its natural environment. For Wright, the beauty of architecture was in how it harmonized with its surroundings.

Wright used many modern materials to achieve his stylistic and personal ideals. Falling water is built largely of reinforced concrete. Wright avoided purely decorative styles of architecture, because he believed that form follows function. In other words, the shape of a building flows from the way it is to be used.

Falling water was designed in 1936 for Mr. and Mrs. Edgar Kaufmann. It is located at Bear Run near Pittsburgh, Pennsylvania. When he was asked years later how he related the site to the house, Wright replied:

"There in a beautiful forest was a solid high rock-ledge rising beside a waterfall and the natural thing seemed to be to cantilever [project outward] the house from the rock-bank over the falling water. . . . Then came Mr. Kaufmann's love for the beautiful site. He loved the site where the house was built and liked to listen to the waterfall. So that was the prime motive in the design. I think you can hear the waterfall when you look at the design. At least it is there and he lives intimately with the thing he loves."

The public did not accept Frank Lloyd Wright's ideas quickly, but years later Mr. Kaufmann said to Wright: "Frank Lloyd Wright, I have spent much money in my life but I never got anything so worthwhile for it as this house. Thank you."

LOOKING AT NATURE
THROUGH CRAFTS

Nature has long been a source of inspiration to the craftsperson. In this section we will look at three examples of useful objects which derive their form and meaning from nature.

Toward the end of the nineteenth century, an arts and crafts movement developed in England. This movement was formed to show that art should be both beautiful and useful. Its members worried that the world of the artist-craftsperson was being destroyed by industrialization. They fought for a return to standards of beauty and craftsmanship that had existed in earlier times, particularly during the Middle Ages.

The "Pimpernel" wallpaper was produced by William Morris, one of the leaders of the English arts and crafts movement. It is a repeating pattern of leaves and blossoms based on linear rhythms. The forms appear to dance about one another. If you stand far away from the pattern, it appears to be just shapes and colors. Imagine the delight of someone approaching a wall papered with "Pimpernel" and discovering that it is almost alive with plant forms.

Figure 72. A detail of wallpaper by the British designer William Morris. (1876)

Figure 73. The function of Louis Comfort Tiffany's *Vase* is reflected in its natural form. (circa 1900)

The glass vase made by Louis Comfort Tiffany looks like a flower. Forms invented by Tiffany were sometimes strange and fantastic, sometimes elegant and simple. Which words would you say describe the vase in the illustration? From a small base a narrow stem rises, opening out broadly into a flower. What kind of flower is shaped like this? A morning glory? A petunia?

The exquisite color and texture of this flower are not to be found in any garden. Tiffany developed a process that would give to his glass pieces a glowing luster. This sheen was like that found on long-buried objects which had been subjected to centuries of erosion and the action of mineral salts. During blowing, Tiffany's glass was exposed to metallic vapors and other chemicals. These gave the finished pieces unusual streaks and textures. Tiffany's glass objects often take graceful flowerlike forms such as the vase shown.

The English arts and crafts movement developed into a broader movement which produced arts and crafts with a new look. This movement was called Art Nouveau, which means new art. Art Nouveau was popular in the early part of this century.

Objects created during the Art Nouveau period display fantastic combinations of form and function. For example, look at the design for the 1925 French automobile *5 Chevaux* (*Five Horses*). The designer, René Lalique, created a mythological animal, joined together and built to fly. This car emblem defined the function of the high-flying automobile. Sometimes Lalique used colored glass as materials for the emblems for car hoods. It must have been quite a sight to have seen a little watery-green frog disappear into the night.

Figure 74A. *5 Chevaux* (1925) *(Five Horses)* **by French designer René Lalique, designed as an ornament for an automobile hood.**

Figure 74B. Lalique's *Glass Frog.* **Also designed as an ornament for the hood of an automobile.**

Can you think of other surprising combinations of form and function that take their inspiration from nature?

LOOKING AT NATURE THROUGH DRAWINGS

For many artists a drawing is a starting place, the first expression of an idea. For other artists a drawing is the idea, a finished work of art. Often, artists paint pictures based on their drawings. The artist Vincent Van Gogh made drawings based on his paintings.

Whatever purpose an artist has in making a drawing, this form of expression has a power of its own.

The two drawings *Rocks in the Sea* and *Sea Forms* present very different approaches to the seascape. The artist Karl Schrag used a brush and black ink to create *Rocks in the Sea*. The strong, energetic strokes in this drawing suggest the power of both the rocks and the swirling sea.

Karl Schrag must have had a very intense response to what he saw when he looked at the rocks in the sea. His powerful brushstrokes reveal that he almost "attacked" the paper in his excitement. So strong is the drawing, *Rocks in the Sea*, that it almost appears that the sea is flexing its rocklike muscles. The sea and the rocks are one—a great weight of mighty rhythms.

The artist William Baziotes approaches the sea in yet another way in his drawing *Sea Forms*. He has chosen for his medium, pastels, or colored chalks. *Sea Forms* goes under the water to look at a world we normally do not see. Strange images float about in this mysterious space. Unlike *Rocks in the Sea*, which suggests that we keep our distance, *Sea Forms* invites us to come close and peer at its interesting forms.

Although Baziotes uses flowing lines as does Schrag, he does so with an entirely different effect. With the edge of his chalk he draws out the fine lines that flow from a nucleus-like center at the top left of the drawing. Because the particles of chalk spread slightly on contact with the texture or "tooth" of the paper, the line has both a sharp and slightly soft appearance. This adds to the mystery of the image. Compare the fine, fluid, soft, and somewhat controlled lines of Baziotes to Schrag's lines. Do you see that Schrag's lines are broader and have a splashier look?

Figure 75.

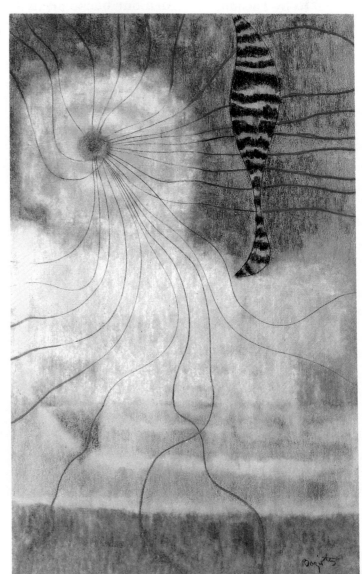

Figure 76.

Figure 75. Karl Schrag used
bold lines and natural forms
in *Rocks in the Sea* (1963).
Figure 76. William Baziotes
depicts a strange and delicate
world in *Sea Forms* (1951).

We have seen that some artists, such as Pieter Brueghel, look at nature from a great distance. Others, such as Albrecht Dürer, show us nature close up, inviting us to study its details. William Baziotes, in *Sea Forms*, takes us closer still. It is almost as if we were looking through the lens of a microscope at sea creatures we could not otherwise see. Or perhaps Baziotes invites us to look with him into the world of our imagination, where anything can dwell. What do you think *Sea Forms* is about?

The artist Theodore Rousseau used a pen and brown ink to draw *Landscape with Farmers' Huts*. His drawing is built up of crisp, short strokes made with the pen. It presents a landscape of solidity and endurance. The movement in this drawing is calmer and less frantic than that in *Rocks in the Sea*. Why is this so? For one thing, Rousseau's drawing does not show the restless sea, but the unmoving land. We can look at it without fear that it will change before our eyes. *Rocks in the Sea* is so full of motion that we might hesitate to turn our backs on it.

Figure 77. *Landscape with Farmer's Huts* **by Theodore Rousseau gives a feeling of solidity to the countryside.**

Figure 78. Richard Parkes Bonington's drawing, *Verona, Piazza del Erbe* is a richly detailed vision of city life. (1826)

Rousseau probably used brown ink, rather than black, in order to soften the effect of his landscape. Brown is a color found widely in nature and would give to the picture a more lively organic appearance than would black.

Rousseau and Schrag each saw solidity and complexity, power and movement, in the land and sea. Each expressed his response in a different way. Each chose the materials, technique, approach to, and arrangement of forms, which would enable him to successfully draw his vision.

The pencil drawing heightened with white, *Verona, Piazza del Erbe*, was made in 1826. It is by the English artist Richard Parkes Bonington. Bonington has used both the point and the sides of his pencil to render a busy corner in a town marketplace. The drawing is done with delicacy, and filled with details such as the facades of buildings and the cluster of people. By merely suggesting details, the artist encourages the viewer to finish the drawing. The viewer therefore becomes involved in the drawing and "sees" more than the artist actually has shown.

The touches of white over the pencil drawing add sparkle and movement, light and life, to the drawing. If we removed the white, the drawing would become flat and less engaging. *Verona, Piazza del Erbe* looks like a stage setting. We see a play unfolding. It is the play of activity among the people and the sunny warmth of the buildings. The buildings and the streets have the appearance of life, of being used, of being worn with activity. It is a friendly and comfortable cityscape. We might even enjoy wandering through the town to shop or to visit with the woman sitting on a bench in the lower right.

Summary Questions

1. What are some of the ways artists capture and hold our attention when we look at their paintings of nature?

2. What is probably the first landscape painting of America?

3. What is a basic shape?

4. Why are brushstrokes important in creating both the look and the meaning of a painting?

5. Why have Far Eastern artists traditionally studied the works of the old masters?

6. Why would an artist such as Barbara Hepworth make works of art that are not clear to us at first glance?

7. How would you compare the photographs of Steichen, Weston, and Muybridge?

8. What is meant by **visual clues**?

9. What is special about Frank Lloyd Wright's design for "Falling water?"

10. Why did a crafts movement begin at the end of the nineteenth century?

UNIT 2

ACTIVITIES

1. Drawing: Position and Attitude   Drawing people is a skill that requires a great deal of practice and concentration. To begin you must first closely observe the position of the figure. . . that is, how the figure is placed and arranged in the setting. Is the person sitting or standing? Is the person slumped or straight? Is the person in a horizontal or vertical position? These are primary and important clues as to how to capture the figure on paper.

After determining position, you'll need to look more closely at the figure to see how the parts of its body are arranged and placed. This is called the attitude of a figure. Are its arms hanging straight down, in the figure's lap, or in another arrangement? Is the figure's head tilted or straight? What about the attitude of the figure's legs? All of these observations are important in trying to capture a figure on paper.

An expression of position and attitude. How does your drawing compare? Student art.

2. Drawing: Expressive Qualities Not everyone you draw will be sitting in the relaxed position of a model. Often you will want to draw someone who is happy, surprised, angry, or frightened. Practice observing and then drawing these kinds of qualities in the face and the body.

Do an exercise in a full-length mirror. (If no mirror is available, work on this experiment with a partner.) Imagine you are frightened. What does your body do? What position and attitude does it take? How does your face appear? Observe yourself in the mirror. (If you are working with a partner, observe your partner looking frightened.) Next try to capture the general position of the body, the attitude of the body parts, and the basic expression on the face. What kinds of lines will you use? Will they be sharp or rounded? Repeat the exercise several times. Each time imagine a different feeling such as surprise, joy, sadness. Make quick sketches for each exercise.

Once you have practiced observing expressive details, you might take your sketchbook to a park or street corner.

Observe people in a real setting. Make quick sketches of the expressive qualities you see.

3. Drawing: Visual Memory   Although you may make many quick sketches of the people and places you want to draw later, your sketches may not record all of the details you want to remember. Sometimes your memory can be the best "sketchbook" of all. But your memory must have practice in observing and recording.

Try these practice exercises. Begin with a large sheet of newsprint. Divide it into four boxes. Then try four visual memory tasks. Look at one part of the classroom for a minute or more. Observe the details of this segment of the classroom carefully. Try to record as many details as you can. Then turn away from the scene and draw it in the first box on the paper. Try to sketch as many details as your memory can retrieve. Number the box 1. The one rule is that you cannot look back at the scene. Repeat the exercise three more times. Each time, change the scene, look at it, turn away and draw, and then number the box. When you finish the four exercises, examine your drawings. Could you remember more details by the time you got to the fourth drawing?

4. Drawing: Light and Shadow   To practice the use of light and shadow in drawing, take a piece of white paper and crumple it gently in your hand. Crumple it only enough to put a few different planes or flat surfaces on it. You may have to try several times before you get one that is not too difficult to draw. Place your form in front of you and draw the figure, paying special attention to the different planes. Draw the lines and shapes of the form. Some of the planes will look light gray and some will look slightly darker. Try to get at least four or five degrees of gray.

5. Drawing/Painting: Toy Animals   Bring a small toy animal to class. Those that come with toy farms or a circus display would be ideal for this activity.

Spend a few minutes looking carefully at your animal. Turn it in all directions. Look at the relationships of one part to another. Are the legs as long or longer than the back? Do the knees bend like yours when you walk? Is the head small? Where are the eyes in relation to the nose?

Position your animal in front of you. On a fairly large sheet of paper and using a felt tip marker, make a large outline drawing with no details. Now, turn the animal a quarter turn in one direction. Use another color marker and make another large outline drawing over the top of the other. Repeat this step two or three more times, turning the animal and using a different color for each drawing.

Look at the composite drawing. You may wish to accentuate some of the lines or fill some of the shapes with different colors or textures, using oil crayons or paint.

6. Painting   Painters achieve the effects in their work through many means. One way is through the kind of brushstrokes they choose. These may be varied in one painting. An artist may use broad strokes in one part of the painting and small dots or points of paint in another part. Experiment with **brushstrokes**.

The materials you need will be several pieces of painting paper, several different sizes of paintbrush, and one color of paint. Look at the brushes you have chosen. What kinds of strokes do you think each brush will make? Experiment and see if you are right. Fill different areas of the painting with different kinds of brushstrokes. How many different kinds can you paint? Do different brushes make different kinds of strokes? Painters usually have many sizes and kinds of brushes. Some are wide and others are thin. Some are very flexible while others are stiff. Compare your brushstroke paintings with classmates. How many different kinds have you made?

Use your brushstroke paintings as guides for the following exercise. On another piece of newsprint, paint each of the following using the brushstroke you think would be the best: waves, snowflakes, billowing sails on a boat, leaves falling from trees, sunset on the horizon, clouds.

7. Sculpture: Imaginary Form   Use your imagination to invent and produce a new animal form. Pretend that you were caught in a storm at sea and the waves that washed over your boat brought aboard a strange new form of sea life.

Collect materials out of which you will make the image of this new form. You may wish to use firing clay or plastic molding clay to produce a model of your strange new find. Then you may want to enlarge the idea. Consider making a papier-mâché enlargement beginning with sheets of rolled newspaper taped into a basic form. (You may need to add some anchors with wire coat hangers.) Wads of newspaper can then be added to give the animal more form. Last, you can apply pieces of newspaper soaked in papier-mâché paste.

8. Sculpture: New Forms   New forms can be invented from various **found objects**. Collect buttons, fabric, plastic parts from packing materials, foil, odd machine parts, and so on. Glue or paste them to one basic shape such as a box, cylinder, or ball. Try several variations before you decide on the final grouping. Several finishing processes may be considered, such as covering all with papier-mâché, or spray painting the whole sculpture one color and adding accent colors.

Mold your own "new form." Student art.

9. Photography: Man versus Nature   Winslow Homer's painting *The Gulf Stream* has as its subject man versus nature. Can you take a photograph emphasizing this theme? Some suggestions might be: taking a photo of a person surfing, riding, skiing, hunting, climbing, sailing, ballooning, fishing, or weathering a storm. You may want to use a faster shutter speed to stop the action. Or try using a slow shutter speed to get an interesting blurred effect. Shoot several ideas or one idea in detail.

10. Photography: Photogram   The essentials of photography are light and light-sensitive materials called emulsions. A camera is not required to make all photographs. Interesting prints can be made using short exposures with a

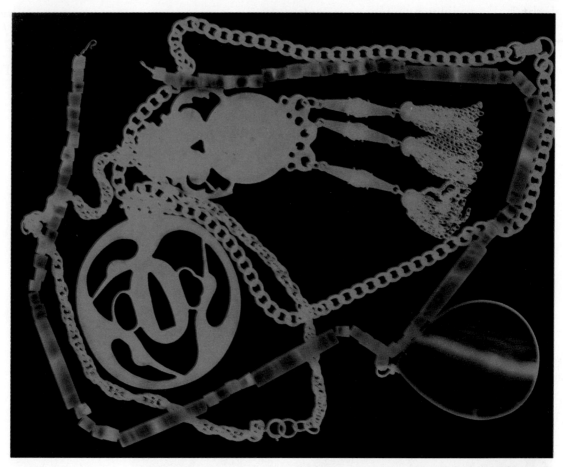

Photography: Man versus Nature.
Student art.

Another photograph in color.
Student art.

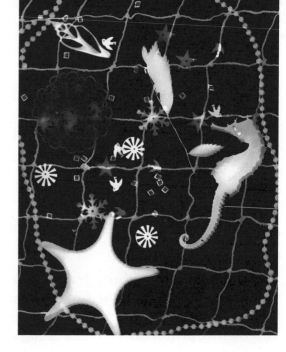

Photogram.
Student art.

light bulb and found objects in contact with an emulsion (photographic paper or blueprint paper). Make a photogram. Begin by collecting some manufactured objects such as cut glass dishes or objects, jewelry, net, lace, transparent projector bulbs, small crystals, dry pasta, textured glass, string, or paper stars. In a pitch-dark closet or room, place these objects on light-sensitive photographic paper. Turn on the light for a few seconds. Next develop, fix, and wash the paper using Dektol. Ask your teacher for more information about these processes. What effect did you achieve? Try a similar photographic experiment using natural objects such as leaves, weeds, flowers, seashells, fan coral, or feathers. How do the two photograms differ?

   If photographic equipment is not available, you might try a similar experiment on a copying machine. Place your objects on the glass of the copier. Push the print button. What kind of image appears? How do you think it differs from a photograph?

11. Fabric Weaving: Pattern   Some art works emphasize all-over pattern. This is referred to as shallow or decorative space. One of the most important uses of this principle is in the designing of fabric. After you have reviewed with your teacher the idea of all-over pattern, experiment with ways of altering the weave of a small piece of burlap. Begin by using a pointed instrument. Alter the weave of the fabric by pulling out threads and reinserting them in different places to produce an all-over pattern.

12. Crafts: Masks   Find pictures in the library of clown faces. Select a clown face that you would like to create in papier-mâché. Your mask will be built on a base made from a strip of newspaper folded and fastened into a ring. The ring is filled with small pieces of crumpled newspaper. Cover the base with strips of papier-mâché. Build up at least four layers and allow them to dry before you build up the features of your clown face. You can use parts of egg cartons, folded pieces of light cardboard, and any other material that will serve as a base for your features. Add ears, nose, eyes, etc., and cover the entire face with five layers of papier-mâché. Allow the mask to dry thoroughly. Now you are ready to paint. Use the clown face that you selected as a guide. Add your own original touches as well. Add yarn for hair and beards.

Figure 79. Papier-mâché clown masks.

Mask.
Student art.

13. Bookmaking In most books, each page is printed on both sides, like your textbooks, and then sewn or glued together at the spine. But, not all books are made this way. Some old Japanese books are not sewn at all, but are made from one continuous sheet of paper that is folded like an accordion or a fan. The cover is also folded so that the body of the book fits right into it and is held secure. In this method, unlike that of your textbooks, you see only one side of the paper.

In this project you will work in a team to write and illustrate a story. Your teacher will duplicate the pages so that each of you can have a copy of the finished product. Then, you will put together your story in the old Japanese manner.

Team up with three of your classmates. Work together to create an interesting story.

Before writing your story, look at some storybooks in the library. How did the authors combine pictures with the story? How large is the writing? Where is it located on the page? Where are the areas of white and where are the illustrations? Notice that the writing and the pictures work

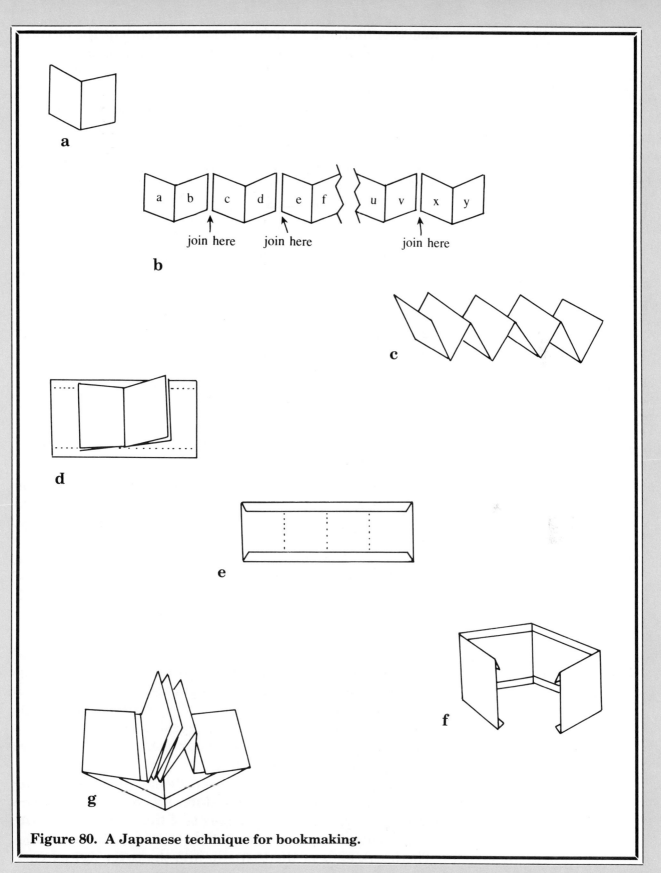

Figure 80. A Japanese technique for bookmaking.

together to create a whole. The story depends on the pictures and the pictures depend on the story. Looking at other books will give you some ideas as to how to actually arrange your story in a book format.

The next step is to plan what part of the story will go on each page. You might make a small outline diagram showing each page of the book as a box. Under each box write the narrative that will go on that page. Add a title page and several extra blank pages in case you want to add to the story. In addition, sketch in or write in a drawing that will go on the page. Number each page.

Once your book outline is figured out, you can proceed with the final production of your book. Cut pages 5 x 7 inches or smaller. Cut as many pages as you have outlines on your diagram. Use only a black felt tip pen to write on each page. Use only one side of the paper for a finished drawing. Number the pages. On the title page add the authors' names, the date, and the city in which you live.

Your teacher will collect your stories and make enough copies so that each member of your group will have a complete copy of the book. The book will be arranged so that two pages fit side by side on an 8-½ x 11-inch sheet of paper. They must fit together as follows:

(a) blank
(b) title page
(c) blank
(d) first page of story
(e) page two
(f) page three
(g) etc., continue pages until end of story

Have the last two pages in the book blank.

When the pages have been duplicated on 8-½ x 11-inch paper, fold each in half inward. With a strip of tape, join the pages as in *b*, back to back. When pasted together the book should resemble *c*. The body of your book is now ready to be slipped into the cover.

To make the cover, start with a sheet of paper about one inch larger on the top and bottom, and about four inches larger on each side than the pages of the book. (*d*) Fold the top and bottom as shown in *e*. Fold the sides inward as in *f*. The blank ends of the text slip into the cover. (*g*)

14. Crafts: Ceramics/Pottery   Working with clay can be satisfying and fascinating. Try this activity for making a textured tile. It introduces the idea of all-over pattern into clay.

You'll need two balls of moist clay and a flat working surface. Press the clay out flat on the surface and then roll it smooth with a rolling pin. Use a dull knife to cut the clay into a tile-sized square. Then experiment with creating textures on the tile. Use your thumb and fingers to make impressions. Try other objects to make impressions such as a pencil, a spool, rubber bands, paper clips, a fork, the decorative handle of a fork or spoon, and so on.

15. Know About Art: Recognizing an Artist's Style   Certain specific works of art can be recognized as being done by a particular artist. That is, you can learn to recognize the work done by some artists even though you may never have seen that work. Look at the ten works of art displayed on the board. Can you pick out those that were done by Winslow Homer? Tell the class why you think all three of the ones you picked were painted by Homer.

16. Know About Art: Style   Some works of art are similar in style. Style can be defined as groupings or classifications of works of art by time, region, appearance, technique, subject matter, and theme. Start a class file of different styles of art collected from magazines, newspapers, calendars, photos, etc. With classmates, decide upon categories in which to file the pictures. You may want to consult art books to find out what style names exist. Why not even create some of your own?

THE ILLUSION OF SPACE

When artists create works of art, they very often must solve problems. The problem may deal with how to draw a particular way, paint a certain apple, or carve a body bending over. These are problems of representing something real, something that we can see.

Other problems may deal with how to express anger, or love, or sadness, or joy. Artists solve problems such as these by the way they show people's faces, posture, and gestures.

Artists also try to solve problems of design. They either try to work within the principles of design or to see how far they can break the rules of design and still make successful works of art. When we analyze works of art using principles of design, we are really playing a game with the artist. We are trying to see how well the artist solved those particular design problems.

Representation, moods or emotions, and design are all art problems that you may also have tried to solve in your art classes, or at home. These are all problems which artists have tried to solve for hundreds or thousands of years, and which every student of art must learn to solve for himself or herself.

The history of art is also the history of how artists in different centuries, in different countries, and in different cultures solved the same problems. Even so, a nose in ancient Egyptian art is not greatly different from a nose in Chinese art. An apple by a Dutch painter of the fifteenth century is not totally unlike one by an American still-life painter of the nineteenth century. Although some differences of style, brushstrokes, or use of color exist, the differences are not complex.

However, there is one problem with which artists and art students have struggled for thousands of years. Ancient Egyptian artists approached it one way, while Greek artists almost two thousand years later looked at it quite differently. Third-century Romans solved it differently than fifteenth-century Romans. Artisans in medieval Germany came up with highly different solutions than the ones used by artists living in the same century in China or Japan. Do you know what that problem is? It is the problem of space! It has been one of the hardest problems to solve in art.

How do you paint or draw something you can't see? Space is something you can walk through, reach out into, but cannot touch. We can only see space because of the objects in space and the distance between them. For example, we can see how far apart houses are or how close trees are to houses. We see space in distance—the distance a road takes to disappear in the landscape, or the distance across a room or swimming pool, or the distance from the front corner of a building to the back corner. The problem of showing space is really one of showing distance as it goes away from us. This is called the third dimension. It means the depth in space.

Dimensions Are Measurements

The first two dimensions are height and width, the third is depth, and the fourth dimension is time. In reality we can measure each dimension, but in art they are illusions. An illusion is a mistaken idea of reality. Perhaps the most magical of these illusions is space, or distance. A painting can give the illusion of distance so great we think we can see for miles and miles, and yet the surface of the canvas is less than an eighth of an inch thick.

The first attempts to create the illusion of space date back to cave painters 15,000 years ago. To show a group of reindeer in a herd, these painters arranged the animals so they overlapped one behind the other. Ancient Egyptian artists used the same overlapping device to show groups of warriors. The Egyptian soldiers marched on a straight line which represented the earth—the soil, the land. In the following three examples, we can see this line.

In the first example, we see a row of lancebearers. Their bodies are twisted flat. The left legs are all forward in a regular pattern, but only the right leg of the first lancebearer has been included. There is no real space between them. Only the ground line is there, which we call a baseline.

Figures 81A and B. Both illustrations show ancient Egyptian lancebearers in an overlapping perspective. Figure A is a modern rendering of the ancient Egyptian infantrymen and figure B is an ancient stone relief.

In the second example, the sand painting of a Navaho, the baseline is below the four figures, but they are not standing directly on it. The four dancers stand above the baseline. Their long thin bodies are bordered by an even longer figure. The head of this figure is on the left, but the feet and legs are on the right.

The third example (Figure 83) is a drawing by a first grader. The student has used the same baseline idea as the ancient Egyptian artisan and the Navaho sand painter. This is a very natural way to draw the earth. By the time most boys and girls are seven years old, they have begun representing the world around them with a line at the bottom of the page.

The Egyptians also used a similar base line to show distance. They merely repeated the same symbol for earth. In Figure 84a, there are two rows of wheat gatherers, or farmers. In reality the top or second row would be *behind* the first

Figure 82. Four ceremonial Navaho Indian dancers. Sand painting from the Nightway.

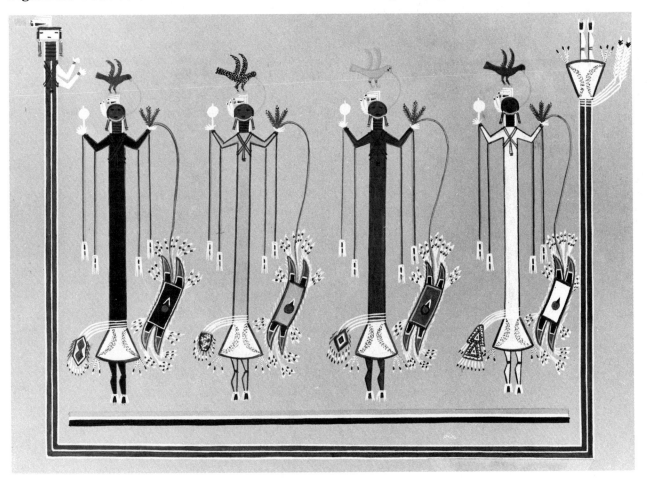

Figure 83. Drawing by a first grader.

Figure 84A. Egyptian wall painting from an ancient tomb in Thebes from around 1450 B.C.

row, but the artist painted the second row *above* the first row. Also, although the artist may have seen that the wheat gatherers in the second row appeared smaller than those up close, he knew they were really the same size. So he drew them as he knew them to be, rather than as he actually saw them.

If one line is called a "baseline" in art, what do you suppose two of them are called? Yes, a *double baseline*, of course. Perhaps you have a younger brother or sister who draws people and objects on double baselines. (Figure 84b is an example of a doublebase line drawing by a first-grade student. Notice how the figures and objects are lined up on one row or the other.

In each of the examples so far, the artists drew what they knew about the objects, not what they saw. They were drawing from imagination and memory. This is more clearly shown in the next examples.

Figure 84B. Children's art illustrating double baseline.

Figure 85A. A pond as illustrated by an ancient Egyptian artist (from a tomb painting).

In this picture we see a garden pool in an Egyptian tomb in Thebes. Notice how the pool is drawn as if the artist saw it directly from above. However, the trees are flat. They are laid out around the pool upright on top, laid out left and right on each side, and upside down at the bottom. The fish and water lotus are seen from the side, the pool is seen from the top.

The artist drew a concept or idea of the fish and the pool. The concept was what the artist knew of a pool and what he knew a person looked like. Such art is called a *conceptualization* because it is drawn from a mental concept, rather than what the artist really saw.

The next example shows a swimming pool by a British artist, David Hockney. Hockney has been painting a series of works on swimming pools. In the drawing below, we are looking at the pool from one end. What do you notice? There are wiggly lines for water. You can see the edge of the pool and the water line, and the walk around the pool and bushes beyond it. But also notice that the pool is narrower at the back end than in front. The left and right sides of the pool slant toward one another near the far end of the pool. In this picture, Hockney drew what he saw, not what he knew.

Figure 85B. *Swimming Pool* by David Hockney.

Is this pool the same shape as the one in the Egyptian painting? Yes, both pools are rectangular, but how differently the artists have treated them.

Notice also that there is no front edge to Hockney's pool. We see the pool through the eyes of the artist. He is looking at the pool. Where might he be? He might be standing on the edge of the pool, or perhaps out on a diving board, or even sitting on the board. Somehow, we know that the artist is there.

Now look at the Egyptian pool again. Where is the artist? To draw the pool as he did, he would have to be directly above it. However, to draw the trees as he did, he must change position. To draw the trees above the pool, he must be below it. Where must he be to draw the trees at the near end of the pool? Where must he be to draw the trees on the right side? The left? The artist must be in five different places to show us the Egyptian pool as he has done. These positions are called *points of view*. In the drawing by Hockney, the artist is standing in a single place with one point of view.

Have you ever drawn a picture like one of these? Think back. You may have without realizing it. It's a very popular way of solving the problem of three-dimensional space.

ARTISTS AND THEIR MATERIALS

It is from nature and the products of the earth that artists get their materials. When the first cave dweller picked up a piece of burnt wood to make a mark on a cave wall, he or she discovered charcoal. The bison and bulls these prehistoric artists painted on the cave walls were of reds, browns, yellows, and blacks because those were the colors of the earth they used to make their paints. They took lumps of soil, ground it, burned it, and then mixed it with perhaps bison fat, honey, or milk to make the paints stick to the cave walls. The cave wall itself was a part of nature. The cave dwellers used the curves and bulges of the wall to form the curves and bulges of the animals they painted.

THE FIRST MATERIALS

What other materials did the cave dwellers use? Their brushes were probably sticks with animal fur or birds' feathers tied to the ends. Archeologists have found small pieces of solid-color material, cut in long straight pieces that may have been used as we use chalk. These early artists used clay from the earth to make small statues for their rituals. They also chipped stones with other stones to make cutting and carving tools. They then decorated pieces of bone and reindeer antlers with geometrical shapes or animal figures.

How else did the cave dwellers make marks? They put their hands on the cave walls, then blew powdered colors through hollow animal bones around their hands. The result: human handprints that have lasted thousands and thousands of years.

So when, as a child, you picked up a piece of charred wood and drew with it on the sidewalk, you were repeating an act many thousands of years old, the act of artists responding to the gifts of nature by drawing, or painting, or sculpting.

THE THREE ELEMENTS OF PAINTING

The history of art has many histories within it. One of these is the history of how artists discovered new materials in nature and then how they invented ways to use them in making art.

To create a painting, you need three things: paint, a brush, and something to paint on. What the artist paints on is called the *ground* or *support surface*. The paint is the *pigment* mixed with a *binder* and applied with a *medium*. Pigments are the colors ground into powder. The binder is the oil or glue which holds the powder together. The medium is the additional oil or water which mixes with the binder or wets it, in order to apply the colors to the support surface. The brush is the *tool* which makes it possible to move the pigments around on the support surface. The tool can also be a stick, a flat blade such as a palette knife, a sponge, your fingers, or anything else that works. Some materials, such as chalks, pastels, crayons, and pencils, combine the pigment with the tool in one piece. Then the tool becomes its own medium. So, the three elements you need to create art are the *support surface*, the *medium*, and the *tool*.

Throughout the centuries, artists have solved the problems of how to combine new pigments with the right binders and mediums, and apply them to the right surfaces to make them last. Some have succeeded better than others. Cave paintings have lasted for hundreds of thousands of years. An ancient Egyptian portrait in wax on a mummy looks as fresh today as in the second century A.D. when it was painted. Still, even the greatest artists have sometimes failed in solving this problem. Leonardo da Vinci painted *The Last Supper* in 1495-1498 (see Figure 86). The painting, in Milan, Italy, is almost constantly being repaired and restored, because Leonardo's experiments with pigments did not work. Because of this problem, an important profession in the art world today is that of restoring and conserving works of art.

Figure 86. *The Last Supper* by Leonardo da Vinci, a fresco in the refectory Santa Maria della Gracie in Milan. (1495–1498)

MAKING COLORS

Artists have always used what they could get from the earth (minerals, soils, plants, shells, gemstones) with whatever skill or technology they had available. Until industrial processes could make colors and pigments from minerals and chemicals, colors produced from natural sources were often rare and costly. Purple dyes were obtained from rare shellfish perhaps as early as 1300 B.C. Purple was so expensive that only kings and emperors could afford to wear it. As a result, purple became a sign of royalty. Earth colors were easily produced from the soils around the Italian cities of Sienna and Umbria. As a result, two popular earth colors are called sienna and umber. Ultramarine blue originally came from lapis lazuli (lap'-is laz'-u-lee). This rare and beautiful gemstone was worn by Inca kings in South America and pharaohs in Egypt. It was very costly to use for painting. Today ultramarine blue can be made by chemicals (sodium, sulfur, and carbonates) and is commonly found in school watercolor boxes and wax crayons.

DIFFERENT STROKES

The art of each age is limited by the materials that the artists are able to use. Fourteenth-century Italian artists used egg tempera (egg yolks mixed with special varnishes and dry pigments). It was a slow, precise painting process. The artist used small brushes to make tiny brushstrokes. An example is this illustration of *The Temptation of Christ* by Duccio (Figure 87). It is only 17 × 18-½ inches.

Compare Duccio's painting with the effect of El Greco's *View of Toledo* (page 71). El Greco painted this in oils on canvas about 1600. The exciting sweep of the brushstrokes, and the sudden darks and lights could never have been achieved in egg tempera, or any slower painting process.

Figure 87. *Temptation of Christ* by Duccio, a detail from the predella of Maestà, in Sienna, Italy. (1308–1311)

Now look again at Van Gogh's *The Starry Night* (page 56). By 1889, when Van Gogh painted this, oils were packaged in tubes. Such paints gave Van Gogh a heavy, thick paint quality not possible in El Greco's time. Once, as Van Gogh wrote in a letter to his brother Theo, he pushed his tube of paint into the canvas at the base of a tree and dragged it upward to get the feel of the tree growing from the earth.

Nowhere in Western European art do we find paintings in ink and brush with the same thick-thin, delicate quality as in the Japanese and Chinese paintings on pages 68–69. How different these are from the strokes used by Franz Kline when he painted *Mahoning* in 1956. Like Kline, many artists began to use house paints and wide house-painting brushes after World War II (1939-45). Such materials seemed appropriate in a highly industrialized age. They were also very useful for the oversize paintings that many artists began producing. Kline's *Mahoning* is 6 feet 8 inches by 8 feet 4 inches.

Figure 88. *Mahoning* **by Franz Kline was painted with a wide housepainting brush. (1956)**

NEW MATERIALS

In the 1840s a company called Windsor Newton invented the collapsible tube. Oil paints and watercolors packaged in collapsible tubes made it possible for artists to paint outdoors. Before this, they had to mix their colors in pots or dishes in their studios. Now, they could easily carry their paints outside. They could paint surrounded by nature, capturing the effect of sunlight on trees, buildings, meadows, and haystacks or recording the effect of fog or cloudy skies. Before, artists had made notes and sketches outdoors and took them into their studios for the final paintings.

The word "pencil" comes from a Latin word *pencillus*, which can be translated as "little brush." The ancient Romans and Greeks used pieces of lead as pencils. In 1564, another writing substance, graphite, was discovered in England. It wasn't until 1795 that a Frenchman named Nicolas Jacques Conté invented a graphite pencil with wooden sides similar to the kind we use today. At first, like the pen and ink, the pencil was designed simply as a writing instrument. But like pen and ink, the pencil was soon used by artists for sketching and drawing.

Wax crayons were actually invented as toy items for children. As the story goes, a peddler in Massachusetts in the 1880s sold colored chalks along with stationery items to homes and stores. However, many mothers would not buy colored chalk, because it got ground into their carpets when children lay on the floor to draw. So the peddler went home, mixed powdered colors with various mediums, and finally used wax. The result: Crayons! They were so popular that children began taking them to school, and finally schools began buying them as part of their regular supplies.

The first boxes of pan watercolors were introduced in this country in the late 1800s by a German immigrant named Louis Prang. Until then, watercolors came in tubes and were just too expensive for school use. Also up until that time, children were only allowed to use pencils or pen and black ink for making drawings in school. Boxed watercolors were inexpensive, easy to carry, and easy to store. They brought excitement and color into the lives of many young artists.

So the history of art is also one of changes resulting from inventions and experiments by artists, and then by manufacturers in making art materials. The artists of the past who made their own materials from nature, who ground the powders and mixed the mediums, grew to love and respect the materials they worked with and to care for them. They were precious and rare. These artists learned to let their materials speak to them, to know what they could do and could not do. They learned not to be impatient with slow-drying mediums and to work quickly with fast-drying mediums. Artists have also learned to take care of their tools, so that their tools will work for them. The artist knows that every surface, every pigment, binder, and medium, and every tool has its own natural laws, which must be respected. There is a secret which all artists have always known: there is something magical about art materials—they make art.

Summary Questions

1. List all the types of arts and crafts materials—surfaces, binders or mediums, and tools. How many different kinds are you using? Classify them according to:

    a. those made entirely by industrial or chemical processes

    b. those which combine industrial and natural products

    c. those which are entirely produced from natural sources

    Which group has the largest amount? What kinds of art or crafts are made from this group?

2. What three elements do you need to make a painting?

3. Why did purple become a sign of royalty?

4. Why does Leonardo da Vinci's painting *The Last Supper* have to be restored so often?

5. The use of chemicals in art materials has rendered some of them toxic for use. Read the list of ingredients and directions for use on your arts and crafts materials. Discuss the proper use of these materials with your teacher.

6. Why is it important for artists to know and understand the materials they use?

7. If you want your art materials to do their best for you, then you must do your best for them by treating them well. Discuss the proper care, use of binders, and cleaning agents with your teacher.

U N I T 3

ACTIVITIES

1. Drawing: Light Light, dim or bright, faraway or near, natural or artificial can affect the way an object or scene looks. Observe how. Place an object on the model stand so that it can be viewed from many different perspectives. Each member of the class sees it from a slightly different point of view. Next, turn a spotlight on it and look at it with this change of light. Does the object appear changed? In what ways?

Select a piece of white drawing paper. Use a drawing pencil to make an outline sketch of the object.

Move the spotlight to a different location in the room or change the light source. Repeat the outline drawing, placing this one on top of the first. How do they differ?

Use oil base crayons to add color to each of the outline drawings. Look at each drawing and plan an interesting color combination. Add texture or pattern to the background.

2. Sculpture Sculptors use a wide variety of materials to make their sculptures. What are these materials? Browse through the art books and magazines in the classroom and look for examples of sculpture. Or visit a local museum and concentrate on the sculpture there. Record your findings on large-size index cards. Study the details of the sculpture, write down the artist's name, the theme of the piece, and the medium the artist used. Be sure to note the source of your findings (name of museum, book, page number). Cards can be categorized with classmates' cards. Post all cards with sculptures in marble in one section of the bulletin board. Organize similarly with sculptures of wood, bronze, and so on.

3. Ceramic/Pottery: Jewelry   Jewelry can be thought of as a form of sculpture that can be worn. To illustrate this concept, find the supply of art, craft, and museum magazines and mail order catalogues that your teacher has collected. Work with two or three classmates. Choose a kind of jewelry to work with. It could be silver, ceramic, beaded, gold, or other. Cut out pictures of jewelry made from your chosen medium. Make a collage of these pictures. When complete, discuss the collages with classmates. Are some pieces of jewelry more like sculpture than others? Why? What are some of the characteristics of sculpture?

4. Ceramic Jewelry   Make a piece of ceramic jewelry. Begin by making sketches of the piece you'd like to make. For ideas refer to the collages made in the previous activity.

Next, prepare a piece of firing clay about the size of an orange. Look at your sketches. Decide how many parts your piece of jewelry will have. How will you connect them together? On a wire? On a string? On leather? What size holes are needed? (Plan for some shrinkage when the clay is fired.) Could you use different colors of clay? How about stains? You might want to paint the pieces with tempera or acrylic paints. You might even consider incorporating other types of materials after the firing, such as feathers, string, wooden beads, plastic pieces, or found objects.

Finish forming and connecting the clay pieces and fire. Then collect all the components of your piece of jewelry and assemble these together. Model your jewelry or get someone else to put it on so that you can see how it looks. Is it sculpture? Are some parts of it more like sculpture than other parts?

5. Ceramic/Pottery: Imaginary Sea Monster   Create an imaginary sea monster or creature out of ceramic clay. Will your monster be like a sea turtle, fish, or dragon-like creature with textured skin? Or will it be a whimsical creature with many fins, tails, and ears? Let your imagination be your guide. After your monster has been fired or dried, paint it with bright colors contrasted with dark ones.

6. Ceramic Pottery   You have had one or more experiences with clay. At this point you will be ready to try working with coils. To make a coil pot, you simply apply clay coils to a clay base. Follow the directions given.

Step 1.   Practice making a few rolls of clay. Take a moist, pliable ball of clay (about fist size) and roll it on the table top in a back and forth motion. With a little practice you will soon have a round smooth roll. Use the same method to make several rolls. Put these aside and cover with a damp cloth until you are ready to use them.

Step 2.   Flatten a piece of clay so that it is about one-half inch thick and large enough to cut a round or oval shape about four to five inches in diameter. Cut out the shape. This is the bottom of your coil pot.

Step 3.   Using one of your coils, place it lightly on top of the base to determine the length needed to go around the top edge of the base. Where the coil meets, cut the ends diagonally so that they will fit together neatly. Use your finger to apply a very thin film of water on the base. Crosshatch the softened area and lay the coil on top. With a light back and forth motion be sure that the coil sits securely on the base. Use your finger or a rounded tool to rub the clay to the base on the inside and the outside of the base. Be careful not to push the coil over the edge of the base. You want it to come straight up. Take the next coil and place it on top of the first coil. It's a good idea to place the coil so that the ends do not meet at the same place as the first one. Again moisten the top of the first coil and place the second on top. Keep the coils going up straight. If they lean out, then you are pushing too hard on the inside or one of the coils was too long. Continue this operation until you have applied about three or four coils. At this point each coil should still have the rounded shape (much like a log cabin wall).

Step 4   To finish your coil pot, you can choose from two possibilities. (1) Leave the outside and inside of the pot with the coils visible. Smooth the joined areas with a tool and your finger, being careful to maintain the distinct coil surface. Or, (2) smooth the outside and the inside to blend the coils into an even surface. You can accomplish this by pinching each coil with your fingers to achieve the same thickness all over. Be careful to keep the sides straight and not let them *stretch* to the outside. If you feel this is happening, you can correct it by doing the opposite from *stretching*—that is by pushing the clay together. Be careful. A little pressure is all that's needed.

What kind of glaze is this? Student art.

Step 5. Let the pot dry until it is stiff and fairly hard, but not completely dry. Pick up the pot and smooth the bottom edge to form a slightly rounded edge. Use a tool to do a final clean up. Scratch your name or initial in the bottom. Place it on a shelf to dry. (It's a good idea to rest it on two pencils so that air can circulate under the bottom. This will help it dry more evenly.)

Step 6. Your piece has dried and been fired. Select the glaze you wish to use. Apply the glaze, let it dry and refire. Join the rest of the class in the critique of all the work. This is an important step. The information you gather can be applied to your next clay project.

7. Crafts: Stitchery   Create a composition on burlap using colored yarn and different types of stitches. Choose a theme for your composition such as fish, faces, buildings, or birds. Or, you might want to create an abstract design or allover pattern. To begin, make a sketch of your idea. Color in the sketch. Now you will have a plan from which to work. Of course, you can change the plan as you begin to stitch. Before starting on your stitchery, you might want to experiment with kinds of stitches. Make a stitching sampler on burlap. Next draw your idea on the burlap with a magic marker and then fill it in with colored yarns.

Student art.

8. Bookbinding   Make and bind your own sketchbook. First, you must decide how large your book is to be, and whether it will have a vertical or horizontal format. The number of pages depends on what use the book will have.

Stack all sheets together on top of each other. Fold the pages in half (*a*). With a ruler find the middle of the book at the spine. Make a mark horizontally from the edge about one-half-inch long. Now make another line the same length an inch from the top and an inch from the bottom of the book (*b*). Cut a slit at each mark through all of the pages. Be sure to cut slightly in from the spine so as not to cut through the spine.

You are now ready to bind the book by weaving ribbon or string. The ribbon or string must be twice as long as the spine. Starting at the top, weave down through the top slit, up through the middle, and down again through the bottom (*c*). Come around the base or foot of the book and back down through the bottom slit. Weave back up to the top or head of the book (*d*). Secure the two ends with a knot being careful not to pull too hard. Make sure the book will lie flat. If it buckles, you have pulled too tightly on the knot.

You can use the same method of making a cover as described in the bookmaking method in Unit 1. The body of the book slips into the cover in the same way.

9. Photography: Stop Action   Many of the paintings you have studied are shown as a moment of action frozen in time. Use your camera to stop action or freeze motion. Shoot at least twenty frames. Find subjects that have foreground movement and stationary backgrounds. Some ideas are: falling water, dancers, vehicles, games or athletics, playgrounds, or flags in the wind.

When using automatic shutter speed-preferred cameras, choose larger apertures (smaller numbers) which will, in bright light situations, cause the camera to "choose" a fast shutter speed to stop action. Listen to the difference in the sounds of the various shutter speeds as you use them.

Carefully examine your finished photographs. Is the foreground action in each shot clear? Is the stationary background clear? Which of the photographs looks like a moment of action "frozen" in time? Explain why.

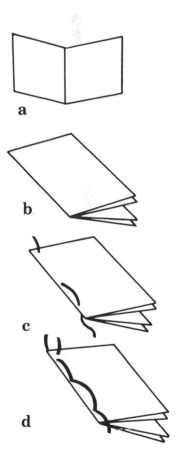

a

b

c

d

Figure 89. Bookmaking.

Stop Action!
Student art.

10. Photography: Water Water occupies a large part of the compositions in many of Winslow Homer's paintings. Water can also be an interesting photographic subject. Water can reflect, magnify, reduce, and distort. Try to take a photograph that has water as the main element. Look for water in various locations—on your window or windshield, on the street in a puddle, in a sprinkler, in a fishbowl or aquarium, in a pool, on the shore, on a leaf, or on a person wearing a shiny raincoat.

Try shooting a variety of shots. For example, you might try shooting a droplet of water up close or reflections in a puddle of water. Show your photographs to the class. Discuss your reactions to photographing water. Did you find it interesting or difficult? Explain why. From your experience photographing do you have some idea of why artists like Winslow Homer often used the element of water in their paintings?

11. Photography: Negative Print Sometimes a film negative looks more dramatic and interesting than its positive paper print. To make a print of a negative image you must make a negative or reverse print. For this process you use a normal prewashed positive print as a paper negative, contact printing it to a fresh (unexposed) wet sheet of photographic paper.

Place the wet positive print face up on a sheet of glass (with the glass edges taped for safety). Next, place the wet unexposed sheet of enlarging paper on top of the positive print, face to face, or emulsion to emulsion. Hold papers with one hand and with your other hand quickly squeegee the two together with a window squeegee to force out air bubbles and therefore make better contact.

Have the enlarger set up for contact printing (largest aperture at a higher height). If you do not have an enlarger, a light bulb will work. Quickly place the glass and paper "sandwich", glass side up, on the baseboard of the enlarger (or on the table under the light source). Do not use an easel. Wipe off the glass with a towel. Work quickly as prints tend to separate. Expose the "sandwich" from one to six seconds. The light passes through the positive print, exposing the negative one. Peel apart and process the reversed or negative image normally.

Here's a negative print. Student art.

12. Printmaking   There are two basic printing processes used in producing multiple images of the same subject. One method is to place ink on a surface and press that surface onto a piece of paper, leaving a mirror impression. This can include simple stamp printing and highly technical etchings and lithographs. The second method is to push or force ink through a kind of screen, usually made of very fine silk or a very strong man-made fiber. A material is applied to the surface of the screen so that no ink can penetrate through the screen.

Printmaking: Repeated Patterns   Simple to very complex "stamp" prints can be produced by using one or more shapes inked and pressed onto a surface. Many different patterns can be achieved by repeating and changing the patterns and by varying the color combinations.

Select or make three different shapes from ½ to 1 inch in size. On a large sheet of newsprint measure and draw a one-inch grid pattern. Using the spaces and only one color, see how many variations of pattern you can achieve. The number can be increased by using more than one color. After some practice, decide on one combination and print at least one sheet using the same repeated pattern.

13. Collographs   Another effective printing process is done by building a print surface from tagboard glued to a backboard (heavy cardboard). Cut out simple positive shapes from a 4 × 5 inch piece of tagboard (save the negative). Glue each to a backboard the same size. Care should be taken with the positioning of the positive and negative shape for proper registration to occur during the printing process.

Using two colors (select complementary or monochromatic colors) produce two different repeat patterns with the same two printing "blocks."

PART

THE ARTIST
IN
THE COMMUNITY

UNIT 4

LET'S GET LOST IN A PAINTING

American Gothic

by Grant Wood

"The land was ours before we were the land's."

Robert Frost

In 1930 an unknown artist submitted a painting to the annual exhibit of new art works at the Art Institute of Chicago. The work caused a sensation and brought him fame overnight. People who never went to museums waited in line to see it. Critics from around the country came to hail "a modern Columbus who had discovered the soul of America." The name of that "unknown" artist was Grant Wood; the title of his painting, *American Gothic*.

FIRST FAMILY IN ART

Fifty years later, everyone recognizes the couple in *American Gothic* as our first family in art. But the agreement ends there. No one agrees why they like it. No one is quite sure what it means. The mystery that surrounds *American Gothic* is one of its fascinations, for while we all look at the same painting we may each see it very differently. Some see comedy, others tragedy, and still others comedy and tragedy. Some see charm, others ridicule, and some even see contempt. And the argument goes on and on . . .

What do you see when you look at this American classic? As you begin the journey to the Midwest (Iowa), take a close look. Can you identify the couple? Are they husband and wife? What are they doing? Thinking? Feeling? Is the picture beautiful? Humorous? Sad? Threatening? Do you see something else? Before you reach any conclusion, keep in mind the strange window and the title, *American Gothic*.

Who does not know these two! Who does not recognize this couple who say nothing, but tell everything about their tastes, their ways, and their beliefs. They are standing in front of their farmhouse as if posing for a picture. The artist-photographer has placed them with objects telling of their work and roles. A pitchfork is in the man's hand and to the woman's left are houseplants. Behind them a lightning rod juts up from a freshly painted farmhouse. In the far background a church spire rises over neatly trimmed trees.

The scene is charming, but the mood is grim. The long faces show their uneasiness. What are they thinking about? They won't tell. Their lips are sealed, closed shut like the blinds of their house. The pitchfork in the man's hand seems to be a warning: Stranger, keep away! Neither of them focuses on the viewer. Their eyes reveal distance. He stares blankly ahead, while she looks to the side. Who are these two? Go back and study their faces closely.

Figure 90. *American Gothic* by Grant Wood (1930).

Most viewers assume they are husband and wife: Mr. and Mrs. American Farmer who carried their Puritan roots from the soil of New England into the rich Midwest farm country. In the portrait the artist-photographer has told a story: Their work is long and hard, their tastes are simple, their religion strict. There is no glamour in their labor and no joy in their lives. The public has always taken them to be husband and wife. Look again and decide for yourself.

The woman is much younger than the man. Her yellow green hair and the soft texture of her skin contrast with his bald head and the hard lines of his wrinkled face. Perhaps she is his daughter or younger sister, but what difference does it make?

To the Iowans in 1930 it made a great deal of difference, so much so that their reaction is part of the strange history of the painting. By mistake, a local newspaper had introduced the work with the title "Iowa Farmer and His Wife," and the Iowans were furious. They thought the artist was ridiculing them. The housewives were angry: "God pity the American farmer if his wife resembled that woman." The artist received so many threats that his mother was afraid to answer the telephone. One local suggested that the painting be placed in a cheese factory "because the woman's face could absolutely sour the milk." Was Wood mocking life on the farm? It is not a happy portrait, nor is it "pretty." Their clothing is immaculately clean but drab. In his Sunday best, he is a sorry figure and she is not elegant. The clothes hide her body, and her figure has been flattened out. Is life on the farm that joyless? Are the good, old-fashioned virtues as dull as this couple appear to be?

THE ARTIST'S VISION

If Grant Wood intended this as a portrait of a husband and wife, the Iowans were absolutely right. The painting could be understood as an attack against a way of life, even against the institution of marriage. If these two were a typical farm couple, the artist was indeed making fun of the rural life. Their relationship became important. When asked, Wood never explained. But his sister did. It was she, Nan Wood Graham, who had posed as the model for the woman. And it was a local dentist, Dr. McKeebe, who had posed for the man. At the time, Nan was thirty-two and the dentist sixty-two.

Figure 91. Photograph taken in 1942 of Nan Wood Graham and Dr. McKeebe, the models for *American Gothic*.

The photograph of these two standing next to the painting was made in 1942, and here they do not look like husband and wife.

As you look at the photograph and the painting, how much likeness do you see between them? If you had been one of the models, would you have been satisfied? Is there enough likeness for the painting to be called a portrait?

The question is not easy to answer, for what is a portrait? Should it be the artist's attempt at an exact likeness of the model, like a photograph taken with a camera? Or should a portrait say something the artist has detected about a person, something in the character? Great portraits reveal character. The art of portrait painting involves constant tension between the artist and model. The model wants the likeness to be flattering. But the artist is looking for a truth underneath the skin—something the model might be hiding. In making the portrait there is a constant battle between how we see ourselves, how we want others to see us, and what the artist sees. When the work is finished and if the client is not happy, what next? This constant pressure to please can force an artist away from portrait painting. Grant Wood once remarked, "If I paint them as they are, what will they think of me? If I paint them as they want to be, what will I think of myself?"

In this case there was no customer, but the good citizens of Iowa mistook *American Gothic* for a portrait of themselves.

WHAT THE PUBLIC SAW

Through no fault of his own, Grant Wood's future in his native state was almost ruined. When the wrong title was published in a local newspaper the people were insulted. Had the artist used the models to reveal some terrible confession hidden in the closets of Iowa? Look at the painting again. Look at the people and the objects. Was the artist ridiculing them and their beliefs?

At first glance this might seem to be a cruel portrait of the "Bible Belt"—deeply religious people who live in the small towns of rural America. The artist included many religious symbols: (1) his shirt suggests the collar of a preacher; (2) her face resembles a Madonna of a Renaissance painting; (3) the window of the house is a church window; and (4) in the background is a church spire. If this is a religious painting the question becomes: What kind of religious belief is the artist showing? The old dress hints at an "old-fashioned" religion. But what do the people actually believe? One writer looked at the painting and thought it meant devotion to a belief in man's God-given right to own property. Look again at the positions of the people and the objects.

The man dominates the space. His placement overlaps the woman, the house, and the trees. If the woman is his wife she is not his equal, but his possession. She is related to the rest of his property. The pattern of her dress is similar to the curtains in the window. Her dark brown dress is similar to the color of the land and the round shape of her head is repeated in the plants and trees.

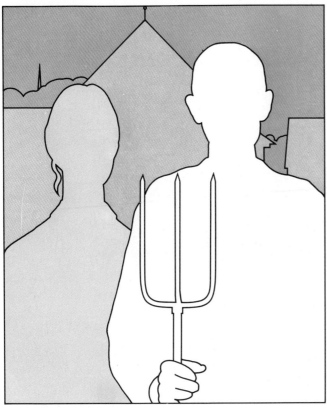

Figure 92.

Figure 92. The outline
shows how the forms in the
painting are related to each
other.

Figure 93. This outline
shows how Wood used
patterns to integrate
different areas of the
painting.

Figure 93.

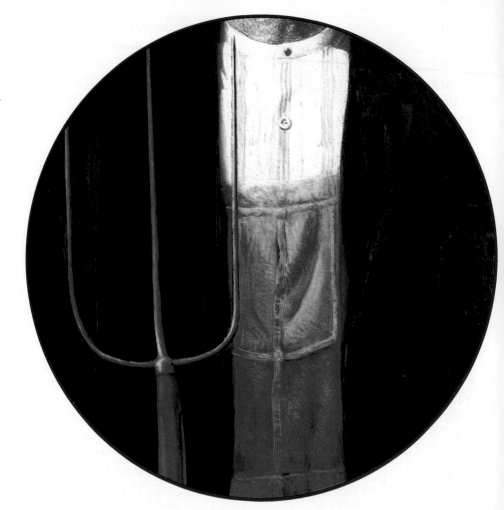

Figure 94. Grant Wood emphasized the pitchfork by repeating its outline.

The man is the dominant person and the pitchfork is the dominant object. The pitchfork is a farm tool, and it is also an instrument of violence. As he holds it in front in his long bony hand, the pitchfork creates tension. The hard look behind the cold-steel glasses could be a warning. His eyes could be fixed on any trespasser threatening him, his beliefs or his property.

The pitchfork has still another, more sinister meaning. By tradition in art, a pitchfork is the sign of evil. Some critics have read the painting in the following manner:

Although this man may go to church—he might even be a Sunday preacher—he is capable of harm. The painting is an attack against people who believe in one thing and practice another. The careful arrangement by the artist is his judgment. The couple seem innocent but they are not. These are people who in the name of virtue do more harm than good. This man's attitude puts the pitchfork in front and the church spire in back. What is this attitude. His belief that everything in his space is his possession. The accumulation of possessions—the material things in life—is more important to him than the Christian values he preaches. Once he defined the pitchfork, the artist played with the tines to complete his effect. The pitchfork has three tines but Wood deliberately added two more points in the painting: the lightning rod and the church spire. If the pitchfork protects the couple from intruders, the lightning rod protects them from the elements, and the church spire guards against modern ideas.

American Gothic has been read as a brutal painting by some critics who feel the couple might be characters from a Gothic story of Edgar Allan Poe. Poe's Gothic stories take place in old settings and are filled with horror and mysterious events. Haunted by some curse of the past, the couple in the painting are doomed in the present. The dreary atmosphere is so stifling that more than one critic wondered how Wood must have suffered at the hands of these people as a young man. No wonder the Iowans were upset by the portrait of "Iowa Farmer and His Wife." Strangely enough, their anger was directed against his portrait of the woman, not the man. If she was miserable and unhappy, no one questioned why. Wood only exaggerated her features. But look what he did to the man. To some critics he made him monstrous. No wonder some artists avoid portraits. The local audience hated what they saw, but for the wrong reason! If the artist had intended only to mock them, how would they have reacted to the true title of the painting?

Once they learned the correct title and identities of the couple, the Iowans went back to look at *American Gothic* again. This time some chuckled, others were deeply moved, but they all saw something that gave them pleasure and pride. What did they see? Take another look at the house. What does it tell about the painting? The title? And if your eye is really sharp, about Iowa?

IOWA GOTHIC

Wood painted the house in 1929 long before he added the occupants. He saw that particular house on an outing in Eldon, Iowa, and it inspired him. He said later that he could imagine the people inside, with stretched-out faces long enough to match the vertical board and batten (a vertical strip of wood used to nail down two boards) lines of the house.

Figure 95. The lines on the house emphasize the vertical movement in the painting.

Roman Arch
Figure 96.

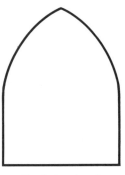

Gothic Arch
Figure 97.

What the artist saw also was the history of a state. For many years what Wood called that "rickety house" had survived the cold of Iowa's winters and its searing hot summers. In the 1860s, when Iowa was first being settled, this was the most popular type of farmhouse in the Midwest. It was called "Iowa colonial" because of its features. The porch was large, and it had a large gable on the roof. The house was made popular by the leading designer of country homes and rural estates, Alexander Jackson Davis. Davis had studied in England and introduced a style called "neo-Gothic" (*neo-* meaning "new"). The word *Gothic* has its own fascinating history. The fifteenth-century Italian writer Vasari first coined it as an insult.

In the late Middle Ages stonemasons found a new way to build arches for cathedrals. The Gothic arch inspired the architects to build churches higher and higher—as if they were reaching toward the sky. Vasari had been used to the more graceful structures of the Roman arch. When he first

Figure 98. This lithograph shows an example of "carpenter Gothic," a style made popular by Alexander Jackson Davis.

saw the medieval churches with their arches and gables, he found them barbaric. He described them as "Gothic," as if built by the Goths, those savage nomadic tribes who brought ruin to Roman civilization. In time "Gothic" was accepted as an important advance in the history of architecture.

Hundreds of years later, the Gothic style became popular in building country homes. Since country architects usually used timber instead of stone, a new term emerged, "carpenter Gothic." Alexander Jackson Davis first made "carpenter Gothic" popular in America. He and Andrew Downing, an expert on gardening, published a series of house designs which they hoped would improve and beautify the American landscape. The drawings were sent out in a catalog and the farmer could select a design and build a house from the plan. The cost was approximately $1,500 from the plan.

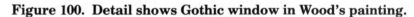

FARMER'S HOUSE.

FIRST FLOOR.　　　　　　　　　　　　SECOND FLOOR.

KITCHEN

LIVING ROOM.
18 by 20

BED　　BED

CHAMBER

"This design is simple, economical and adapted to the American climate. It is two stories high with a garret loft. The porch may continue or stop at the dotted line. The bold gable is an essential part of the design."

Figure 99. Floor plan for "carpenter Gothic" house.

Figure 100. Detail shows Gothic window in Wood's painting.

Although not the one in the plan, this is the type of house Wood saw in Eldon, Iowa. He also saw something else, the window. Notice the Gothic shape of the window. How strange! How did a Gothic monstrosity, this relic from the Middle Ages, suddenly show up in an Iowa farmhouse? What was it doing here in the American Midwest?

THE ARTIST'S PLAN

Wood photographed the Eldon house and returned a few weeks later to do an oil painting of it. Shortly thereafter he made a pencil sketch for *American Gothic* with a couple standing in front. Within a few months he finished the painting as we know it. By looking closely at the photograph, the first painting of the house, and the sketch, you can follow the artist's plan from first idea to the finished work. (Figure 102)

Can you see any difference between the house in the photograph and the one in the painting? Did you notice how Wood heightened the gable to get his "Gothic" effect?

Figure 101. Photograph shows the house in Eldon, Iowa, which Wood used in his painting.

Figure 102. Above is the first painting Wood did of the Eldon farmhouse. The pencil sketch is an early study of *American Gothic*.

american Gothic

In the first painting, he made the gable a little higher and more steeply angled to suggest the Gothic feeling of height. This first effort is the beginning of the artist's exaggeration. Before he stretched the faces of the couple in *American Gothic* he stretched the house, narrowed the gable, and made the window taller and more prominent.

In his first pencil sketch he included a man and a woman in a grid.

Here the hard angles of their faces and their sloping shoulders begin to repeat the angles of the gable. The artist again changed the length of the gable and the window. To the left he added another Gothic arch in what might be another window or doorway. The man is holding a rake. In the final painting the rake became a pitchfork. What does the pitchfork add to the design? Go back again, compare the sketch with the final work, and try to decide why Wood changed the rake to a pitchfork.

You might say the pitchfork is a stronger image for the farmer. It belongs in his hand. But the pitchfork also strengthens the design of the painting.

Figure 103. The finished version of *American Gothic*.

Wood understood the importance of repeating shapes, and the addition of the pitchfork completed the design. The idea for the final design was for the lines of the Gothic window to repeat in the faces. When the Gothic arch is turned upside down, it has the shape of the pitchfork. Before going to the diagram, go to the painting and find where the shapes of the Gothic arch and pitchfork repeat.

The diagram shows how the pitchfork repeats in the bib of the overalls and in the man's face. The three tines of the pitchfork repeat in the window, the hand, and on the sides of the barn and house. The Gothic arch repeats in the woman's hairline. The vertical pitchfork creates the illusion of

Figure 104. The upside-down Gothic window.

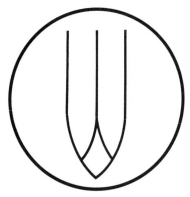

Figure 105. The shape of the pitchfork is repeated in the Gothic window.

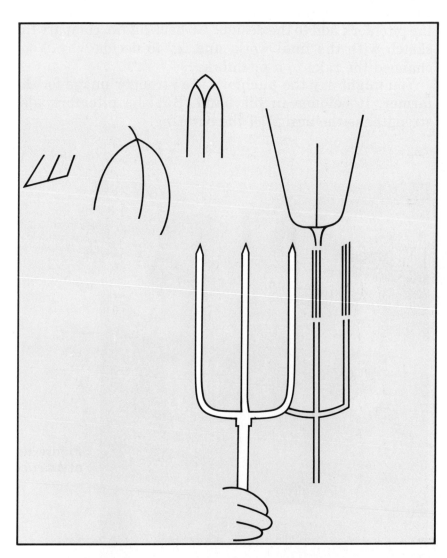

Figure 106. Drawing shows the many pitchfork shapes repeated in the painting.

height. Follow the left tine of the pitchfork. It points upward directing the eye to the lightning rod and the steeple. The design has the feel of Gothic architecture: tall and somber. It is an architectural painting made up of vertical and horizontal lines. It is a static composition, that is, it requires very little eye movement. As the lines meet they form right angles and slow down the eye. The next diagrams show the vertical and horizontal lines of *American Gothic*.

For contrast, and to avoid monotony, Wood used circles, semi-circles, and ovals (the cameo, her dress, the curtains). The circles form diagonal lines which meet at angles.

The pitchfork is the dividing line at the center of the

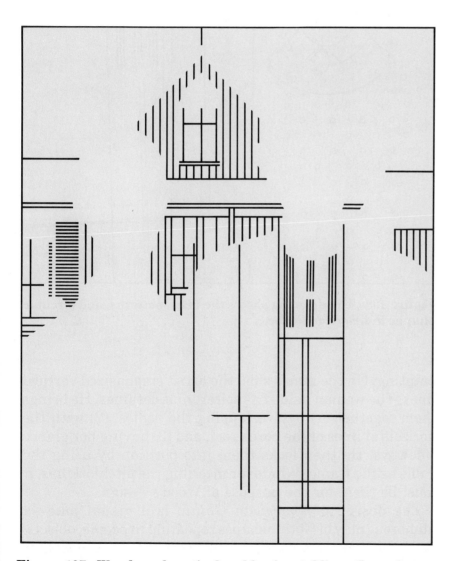

Figure 107. Wood used vertical and horizontal lines throughout his painting.

Figure 108. The drawing shows the lines, patterns, and circular shapes in *American Gothic*.

painting. On the man's side, the artist emphasized vertical lines. The woman's side has softer, rounder lines. He brings them together (1) by overlapping the bodies, (2) with the horizontal lines of the porch roof, and (3) having her glance sideways. He then locks them into position by using the gable as the frame. Whatever meaning the pitchfork has, it must be there for the purpose of Wood's design.

The design of *American Gothic* is a visual joke—a humorous play of Gothic shapes repeating in people, objects, and landscape. But was the artist laughing at the models or with them?

IDEAS FROM THE PAST

Grant Wood was often asked to explain the couple in *American Gothic*. He said he wanted an "elderly spinster type" for the female model, but could not find one. He never said that he intended them to be husband and wife. He did, however, have much to say about "Gothic." In the vocabulary of art, "Gothic" refers to a historical painting style. Gothic art flourished in Europe between the thirteenth and sixteenth centuries. It began as artists started to paint copies of sculpture from Gothic cathedrals. The angular faces and sharp folds of the dress in Gothic paintings were inspired by the sculptor's chisel. According to Wood, Gothic art was the major influence on his work. When he spoke about *American Gothic* he often referred to the fifteenth-century Gothic master Hans Memling. Look at the two Memling portraits . Can you find similarities to *American Gothic*?

Figure 109. Hans Memling *Lady with Pink*.
Figure 110. Hans Memling *Portrait of a Young Man*.

1. The severe expression of the faces.
2. The oval shapes in the landscape—repeating the shape of the woman's head.
3. The prominent hands.
4. The straight lines of the clothes used to frame the face.
5. The similar use of color.

Figure 111. Compare *American Gothic* with the two portraits by Hans Memling.

Although only a few of his works survive, Hans Memling's greatness remains unquestioned. His portraits do not show the beauty of the human body but celebrate the soul of the quiet, pious, and hard-working people of Flanders. Memling was a devout Christian and his paintings are religious statements. They are meant to move the believers to humility before God and toward courage in life. His people have the "Gothic look"—bony faces, severe poses, hard lines, and intense, staring eyes. The hands are important and prominent, clasped as if in prayer. The background landscapes are dreamy pieces of nature hidden in corners of the painting. Figure 111 shows some traces of Memling in *American Gothic*.

As in Memling's work, in *American Gothic* the color (or tonal values) goes from light at the top to dark at the bottom. Since the couple are outside, the colors are natural. The sky and the sun are lightest. The couple's flesh, the man's bald head, and white shirt are also light. Wood places the woman's dark apron and the man's dark coat at the bottom. This weighs the painting down and gives it a firm base. The gray values—the shadows between light and dark—make a slow change rather than a series of contrasts. If the dark colors were at the top, it would be top-heavy. They would press down on the couple and the house, thus changing the mood of the painting.

Memling painted three-quarter portraits, that is, portraits halfway between a profile (or side view) and the full face. In his works the subjects do not look at the viewer because their thoughts are elsewhere. It is almost impossible to read feelings and emotions in their faces; they are

Figure 112. In the Hans Memling portrait, the lighter tones appear at the top, and darker tones appear nearer the bottom.

Figure 113. Compare Grant Wood's use of color tone with the Memling portrait.

distant. Their eyes do not focus on the real world because they reflect some inner drama of the soul. The portraits are votive. "Votive" refers to the fulfillment of a religious vow. The faces of Grant Wood's couple have the same feeling. You are looking at them but they do not see you. Their thoughts are elsewhere. They are removed from us. Like Memling's subjects, Wood's faces suggest a votive painting. These two are fulfilling a vow. But to what? To the Church? To the house? To each other? Or to the most prominent object—the pitchfork? The answer to the question is as mysterious as the faces of the couple. It lies elsewhere in Wood's life and work.

THE ARTIST'S BACKGROUND

Grant Wood was born in 1891 on a farm in Anamosa, Iowa. When he was ten his father died, the farm was taken away, and his family then moved to Cedar Rapids, Iowa. He did odd jobs to support them, and taught himself to paint at night. After high school he studied art and design in Minneapolis and Chicago and served as a soldier in World War I. After the war he taught art for seven years in the Cedar Rapids schools. During this time he made several short trips to Europe to study art and to paint. In 1927 he received a commission to make a veterans' war memorial for Cedar Rapids. The stained glass windows were too difficult to make in the United States, so he went to Munich, Germany, to work with craftsmen long skilled in the art of stained glass.

Munich was the turning point in his life. It was there that he came under the influence of the Gothic artists and especially Hans Memling. Memling's stony looks reminded him of the faces of Iowa farmers he had known; the lovely clothes suggested the patterns of his mother's old dresses; and the delightful shapes of Memling's landscape recalled the rolling hills and neatly planned cornfields of home. Here he was, thousands of miles away, looking at the work of a Gothic master, separated by hundreds of years in time, and what did he see? Iowa!

The Munich trip had become a voyage of self-discovery. Wood had solved for himself a problem that had long bothered American artists—the need to go to Europe. Of course they had to visit the art capitals of Europe and America. Here in the great museums hung the paintings of the masters. But, as Wood learned, they did not have to stay there for inspiration to paint. For almost forty years he had lived as an obscure artist, earning hardly enough money to support himself and his art. Although he would live only twelve years after Munich (he died in 1942), he produced in that short period of time a series of outstanding paintings that live on.

CHANGES IN STYLE

The visit to Munich hastened something that probably would have happened anyway. We cannot know what goes on inside the mind of the artist. But there is the evidence—

his work. In 1928 there was a dramatic change in Wood's style. A typical example of his earlier work is *The Yellow Doorway* (page 168). This work shows the influence of European art, especially Wood's knowledge of the techniques of Impressionism. The thickness of his paints suggests the blazing sun hitting the rough surface of the stonework. This is an important work but very different from his approach to art after his return from Munich. Compare this with his 1929 painting *Woman with Plant* (page 169) done after his return from Munich.

The woman is the artist's seventy-year-old mother. This work is probably his most Gothic painting. Notice the bony hands holding the flowerpot and the face turned to the side. Below, a small winding road, a dreamy corner of nature, leads to corn shocks and a little schoolhouse. Behind the

Figure 114. *The Yellow Doorway* **by Grant Wood (1923) is an early painting.**

Figure 115. *Woman with Plant* by Grant Wood (1929). This painting shows the influence of the Gothic portrait artists.

schoolhouse delicate, round-shaped trees lead to a windmill in the distance. The landscape tells the story of her accomplishments, and contrasts with her severe features. The history of the American pioneer is in the woman's face. She is much larger than the land. Her portrait speaks of years of sweat and toil, of hard winters, summer heat, disappointment, survival, and most of all, courage.

The snake plant in her hand follows another Gothic convention. Gothic artists paid attention to the smallest detail. Everything in a painting is there to express human character and the glory of God. In Memling's time the story behind *The Lady with Pink* (page 163) needed no explanation. The "pink" in her hand is a carnation. It was a Flemish custom for the bride to wear a carnation on the wedding day; the pink expresses the purity of the woman's love. In Wood's portrait the snake plant is an important part of her story. The tropical snake plant is one of the hardiest plants. Its will to survive the Iowa climate reveals the character of the woman. The snake plant and the begonias also appear in *American Gothic*.

In 1930 Wood completed *American Gothic*. There is something strange about this painting in that it is almost impossible to date. It has the feel of another time. Go back to the work again. Is there any way to identify the date of the painting? There are some clues. Wood had given specific instructions to his sister to wear an apron trimmed with rick-rack braid. When she tried to buy it she was told that the stores hadn't carried it for years. She had to tear the rick-rack from one of her mother's old dresses and sew it on the apron, while underneath she wore an old dress. By 1930, even a three-tine pitchfork was becoming obsolete. Her clothes and the pitchfork are from another time. The artist had a specific idea in mind: to make a living image of the past.

Again we can imagine Wood facing Memling. After a while Memling's portraits have a strange and wonderful effect. His people belong either in a convent or a monastery. No matter when they might have lived, there is the feeling

Figure 116. Wood was influenced by the landscapes of Currier & Ives, such as this lithograph titled *Home to Thanksgiving*.

that time passed them by. Wood's couple have that same feeling. Although they live in the present, they belong to the past—the artist's own past. Had he not spent the happiest years of his life on a small farm in rural Iowa? Wood had strong ties with the art and history of the Midwest, and he always had a passionate interest in early American folk art. He loved the solid furniture of early American craftsmen and often furnished and decorated houses in the older style. He collected and studied historical maps and atlases. He loved the pattern of his old family china and the landscapes of Currier & Ives. The charm of these earlier styles appeared in Wood's later works.

He spent hours looking at early pioneer photographs. That led him once to explain that the couple in *American Gothic* were "tintypes from an old family album."

The critic Wanda Corn has shown how the arrangement of the couple in *American Gothic* was actually suggested by the nineteenth-century photographer Solomon Butcher.

This photograph of John Curry's sod house could easily have served as a model for Wood's piece of history. The traveling photographers usually posed a couple in front of their house. The painting has other similarities to the photograph—the dress, the stiffness of the bodies, the unblinking eyes, and stares of the couple. Notice also the plants potted in cans. The indoor plants were a source of pride, since it was hard to keep plants alive during the long winter. A pitchfork identifies the man as a farmer, but it also kept him steady during the long time necessary for photographic exposure.

Figure 117. This early photograph by Solomon Butcher titled *John Curry Sod House* may have influenced Wood.

Figure 118. *Daughters of Revolution* **by Grant Wood (1932). This painting created another uproar among Grant Wood's public.**

OTHER PAINTINGS

When an artist looks into the past, he reveals his feelings about the present. What does *American Gothic* tell about 1930? Is it, after all, a joke—a spoof about people who lived in the past and are ridiculed in the present? Is it one artist's statement against his community of uncultured American Goths? Or were these outdated folks who struggled to keep the plants alive telling us something beautiful and true about a vanishing America? Which definition of "Gothic"— story, art, architecture—applies to the painting? Maybe they all fit. His other works on the following pages show him to be capable of ridicule, *Daughters of Revolution*; humor, *Victorian Survival*; anger, *The Appraisal*; and tender sympathy, *Fall Ploughing*.

Daughters of Revolution (1932) created a storm of protest. The artist previously had trouble with a patriotic organization, the Daughters of the American Revolution (DAR), because of his visit to Germany to finish the stained glass window for the war memorial. Members of the DAR complained that an American war memorial should have been made in America and not in Germany, the former enemy in World War I. The painting is a good-natured slap at the DAR. In the background is Emanuel Leutze's classic painting *Washington Crossing the Delaware*. This time the artist's visual joke is to repeat the prow of the boat in the mouths of this prim and proper threesome. They are celebrating a historic occasion: Washington's 200th birthday in 1932. Wood's idea for the celebration was to place a bony hand making a "dry" toast with a cup of tea. Behind the joke is the artist's resentment of any so-called "aristocrats" in America who would use and abuse the name of George Washington, the leader of the American Revolution and the father of this democracy.

Wood's model for *Victorian Survival* was a tintype photograph of his aunt, Matilda Peet, from his own family album. It is another visual joke. A long-necked woman sits next to a long-necked, old-fashioned telephone. The woman comes from the 1880's—the time of Queen Victoria; the telephone from the 1920's. The telephone and the twentieth century have come, times have changed; but like the couple in *American Gothic* she hasn't. The discomfort is in her face. *She resembles a chicken!*

Figure 119. *Victorian Survival* by Grant Wood.

Figure 120. The photograph that served as a model for the painting, *Victorian Survival*.

Figure 119.

Figure 120.

The Appraisal (1932, original title *Clothes*) is a lesser-known work, but one with a message. Two women meet to discuss the value of a hen. The woman on the right comes from the big city and is elegantly clothed in the furs of a dead animal. Her vicious double chin shaped in the form of a second pair of lips suggests her huge appetite. On the other side a wholesome farm woman embraces the hen. Her clothing is simple and she is at one with the animal, holding it proudly and close to her. The fat hen has a thick, elegant coat—the most luxurious of the three. The hen's look of concern is justified, for it will end up on the table of the city woman. While there is humor in this harmless scene, it is actually a fierce painting. *The Appraisal* deals with the price of a hen, but the artist is also making an appraisal of country life versus city life. The solid farmhouse in the background with its flowering potato patch is life. The city woman is out of place here. *The Appraisal* is full of an artist's venom, ridicule, and contempt. The statement is clear: the farm provides, the city takes. It tells much about the meaning of *American Gothic*.

In many of his works Wood celebrated the virtues of the American farm. One of his best is *Fall Ploughing* (1932).

Figure 121. In *The Appraisal*, Wood contrasted farm people to city people.

There are hints of this work in *American Gothic* where the eye, disappointed by the grim faces of the couple, wanders into Wood's dreamy corners of nature—the landscape. Here is food for the dreamer. The rounded shapes of the plants and the trees rising up like toy balloons are so inviting that we are tempted to remove the people to see what else is there. The artist accomplished this in *Fall Ploughing*. The work is Wood's tribute to a nineteenth-century American invention, John Deere's walking plow. With this marvelous invention, farmers no longer had to stop every few yards to clean the moist topsoil from the blade. It was the "plow that conquered the soil" and made big harvests possible. In the painting the plow stands alone. The clean curve of the blade repeats in the lines of the landscape. You can feel the lift and sweep of the ground. The corn shocks march in formation and the rolling hills glide off into the distance. It is an earthly paradise made by man and his plow.

Figure 122. *Fall Ploughing* is Grant Wood's tribute to the Iowa farmland he loved.

Like *American Gothic, Fall Ploughing* speaks of another time. But could these works have been painted at another time? Go back once more to *American Gothic* and *Fall Ploughing*. Can you determine whether they are nineteenth- or twentieth-century works?

Grant Wood's paintings always began as abstract designs. He once said: "All my pictures are first planned as abstract shapes and only then do I put the clothes on." The exaggerations in *American Gothic* fit Wood's design. In *Fall Ploughing* the corn shocks are all the same size and line up in even rows. To explain the importance of repetition in his design, Wood used to show a photograph of corn shocks which were of different sizes and sagged lifeless to the ground. This insistence on shapes, lines, color, design—what are known in art as the "formal" aspects of a painting—dates him as a modern artist. Although his objects are recognizable, his technique is modern. His fields, his houses, and his people are abstract shapes in the mind before they become objects in his paintings. He is just a brushstroke away from unrecognizable objects—one step away from abstract art. His designs change the landscape into geometric patterns with dazzling repetitions of line and shape. The style is part of the new visual experience that is modern art.

Grant Wood's style does not explain *American Gothic*, but it leads to an intriguing question. Why did this modern, sophisticated artist who traveled and studied in the art capitals of America and Europe go back to the past? Why do his 1930 paintings have people dressed in Victorian clothes with long-outdated tools? By 1930 many American farms had become mechanized. Why is there no modern equipment in his world—no giant harvesters, tractors, or mechanized plows? His farms, like his people, are relics of the past. They existed long before the bulldozer destroyed the American landscape for the expanding cities, long before highways brought the automobile. These paintings are his judgments. His farmers have seen the progress but have not yielded to it. They seem uncomfortable and ridiculous, and their manner might baffle the modern viewer. The artist did not reveal them, but their faces reveal Grant Wood.

Years later Grant Wood wrote about himself and his commitment to the farmer. In his essay "Revolt Against the City" he wrote about the reserved farmer who is ridiculed by city people: "When the gentle farmer is called a hick he withdraws." Wood's farmer was in a never-ending battle against drought, famine, dust storms, heat, and floods, and dealt with the constant threat of losing his farm to the bank. He had no time for idle chatter or posing for slow-speed cameras. Grant Wood's art interpreted the drama of that life. *American Gothic* is a votive work, with two vows fulfilled: the farmer's to the land and the artist's to the farmer.

REGIONAL PAINTERS

With the early thirties came a time of crisis and upheaval in American history. Perhaps the Great Depression, when millions of Americans were out of work and on breadlines, put that look on their faces. Something had gone wrong with the American dream. Most of the art of the Great Depression expresses the fear, suffering, and disappointment of the time. While most American artists were questioning, others had been rediscovering their country. These artists, called Regionalists, had gone back to the soil, the strength of America's past. They left the art capitals of the Western world and went back home: John Curry to Kansas, Thomas Hart Benton to Missouri, and Grant Wood to Iowa. These three took their inspiration from an America that was and is no more.

Figure 123. Thomas Hart Benton, another regionalist painter, shows his attraction to the American way of life in *Cradling Wheat.*

Figure 124. J.S. Curry depicted scenes from life in Kansas in paintings such as this one titled *The Tornado*.

That's not quite true! The couple in *American Gothic* is alive and well. The passage of time has only added to their stature. Although most people have not seen the painting at the Art Institute of Chicago, everyone recognizes it. The couple appear in posters, advertisements, and jokes on the presidential family. They are so much a part of us that cartoons need no explanation.

American Gothic has become America's self-portrait. It remains a large success because a portrait involves three people—the artist, the model, and the viewer. The models say, "The picture does not resemble us." The artist responds, "What do you see when you look at yourselves?" The viewer adds, "What difference will it make a thousand years from now?" The models ask, "Is it us or a picture of us?" The artist says, "Yes." The viewer asks the critics. The models ask, "Who are we? What does the painting mean?" The artist responds, "You are characters from a Gothic novel, living in a Gothic structure as parts of a Gothic painting." You the viewer, still not sure, must go back to the painting one more time. Is the picture beautiful? Humorous? Sad? Threatening? Something else? The obvious answer is yes! It is beautiful because the artist has opened to us a new way of seeing life. It is humorous, sad, yes, even threatening because these words represent essential truths of life.

"If these are truths of life," say the models, "how about the landscape? We never saw such exaggerations." The artist responds, "God made the trees, I can only make paintings." The viewer agrees with both. The models say, "But our clothing is so old." The artist responds, "Your clothing, like you, is timeless." The viewer sees the first and eventually recognizes the second. The models ask their last question: "Are we husband and wife?" The artist just smiles but does not answer. He lets you, the viewer, decide. Now what? The joke is on the viewer. At first the Iowans hated it because they thought the two were husband and wife; now it is universally liked for the same reason. We cannot even ask because the artist locked the couple inside the design. We cannot get in and they have no intention of coming out.

Are we any closer to the meaning of the painting? Although we have not solved the mystery of *American Gothic*, we have come closer to its truth. The enormous popularity gives the couple a living presence—a life beyond the picture frame. "Some life!" mutters the cynic. The couple leap outside the painting and respond, "Look at yourself! Where are your vows? Where is your integrity? Your conscience?" The viewers look again, this time not at the painting but at themselves. And the disagreements continue. . . . Some see charm, some ridicule, and others comedy; for some there is tragedy, for they see nothing.

We wanted to discuss these matters with the artist. By then he had gone on to his next work. . . .

If his later paintings shed light on *American Gothic*, this painting tells everything about Grant Wood. *American Gothic* stands alone among his works. Whether it is a masterpiece remains an open question. It is certainly his centerpiece. All his genius and talent were expressed here. Its style and meaning stamp the other paintings with his vision of America. What was that vision? In 1961 the Vermont poet Robert Frost spoke at the inauguration of President John F. Kennedy. Quoting from his poem "The Gift Outright" he described the American people with the mighty line, "The land was ours before we were the land's." Grant Wood's farmers belonged to the land. They built it so it could be ours.

Summary Questions

1. People and what people do have been favorite subjects of artists since prehistoric times. Portraits have also been a favorite subject matter. Portraits differ from other paintings about people because in a portrait people are usually not doing anything except posing. Usually a portrait title simply says who the people in the picture are. The title does not tell a story or describe something else. In what ways would you say that Grant Wood's painting *American Gothic* differs from the usual portrait?

2. In Part I of this book you read about the ways in which artists have solved the problems of distance and space. One solution was overlapping. Find an example in Wood's paintings in which he used overlapping. Look at the painting *Fall Ploughing* on page 175. How did Wood solve the problems of space and distance in that picture?

3. Artists get their ideas for paintings from many sources. Name three sources which Grant Wood used.

4. What are some of the ways in which *American Gothic* is similar to Hans Memling's *Portrait of a Young Man* (page 163)?

5. How would you describe the colors of *American Gothic?* How do they affect the impact of the painting?

6. In what way does *American Gothic* reflect Gothic architecture? How do you think it reflects a Gothic novel or films?

7. In Part I you read about artists and nature. Study *Fall Ploughing* on page 175. How does Grant Wood portray nature in this painting? What kind of relationship does he imply between people and nature?

8. Grant Wood often used symbols in his work. Name a symbol he used in each of these paintings: *Daughters of Revolution* and *Woman with Plant.*

ELEMENTS
OF
DESIGN

In Unit 1 you learned about the elements of design—color, form, line, texture, space, and value. Let's see how Grant Wood used these elements in his painting, *American Gothic*.

COLOR AND VALUE

The colors in *American Gothic* are mostly dark and somber. Notice how much black and gray Wood used. The lighter colors in the background make the figures seem even starker. There is, however, a triangle of reds in Wood's painting. Can you find it? Start at the red barn on the right side, then move your eye to the woman's brooch. The third angle of the triangle is in the reddish browns of the man's hand. Close your eyes for a moment and try to imagine how Wood's painting would look without this red triangle. Would it be as effective?

The artist also used many values of grays and browns in *American Gothic*. How do these help provide unity to the painting?

FORM

You have read about some of the forms such as the Gothic arch that Grant Wood used. The diagram on page 160 showed you how circles were repeated in many parts of the painting. Look at the picture again. Find the pointed V-shape of the house roof. How many similar shapes can you find in the painting? Don't forget the rick-rack on the woman's apron!

LINE

The diagram on page 161 showed you how Wood used vertical and horizontal lines. These lines, repeated over and over, help to give the painting a sense of stability. We feel that these people will never move; they are there on the land forever.

SPACE

Compare the painting *American Gothic* to Wood's painting *Fall Ploughing* on page 175. Which picture depicts a more vast sense of distance and space? Why? What device did Wood use in *American Gothic* to show that the man is slightly nearer to us than the woman?

TEXTURE

American Gothic is mostly a smooth painting. It does not have the rich textural contrasts that Homer's *The Gulf Stream* does. If you look carefully, you will see some indication of natural textures in the trees and shingles on the porch roof. The texture of the blue coveralls under the farmer's coat is made by small refined brushstrokes. Grant Wood worked in egg tempera and varnish, materials which do not lend themselves to the heavy brushstrokes used by Homer.

PRINCIPLES
OF
DESIGN

You recall that the principles of design are unity, balance, emphasis, movement, variety, and proportion. Let us look at how these principles work in *American Gothic*.

UNITY

A number of elements contribute to the unity of Wood's painting. You have already learned how he used repetition of forms, lines, and colors to create unity. As in *The Gulf Stream*, this painting is also unified by the subject matter or story.

BALANCE

In Part I you learned about the three types of balance: formal or symmetrical, informal or asymmetrical, and radial. What kind of balance does *American Gothic* have? The diagram and text on page 160 will give you a clue.

EMPHASIS

What did Grant Wood emphasize in *American Gothic*? Do you recall how he changed a rake in an early sketch to the pitchfork we see in the finished painting? Wood used the pitchfork to strengthen the design of his painting. He also used it to emphasize the faces of the man and the woman.

MOVEMENT

What principle of design is strong in *The Gulf Stream*, but almost missing from *American Gothic*? You are right; it is movement. *American Gothic* is really a static picture. Everything stands still, while in *The Gulf Stream* everything moves. In Wood's painting the people do not move, the wind is not blowing the trees, the curtains do not flutter in the breeze. The composition with its verticals and horizontals does not move. Still, your eye moves around the picture. It is directed up by the pitchfork and vertical lines. It is carried across from side to side by the white edge of the porch roof. Devices such as the triangle of red color also help to move your eye from one part of the picture to another. The woman's face and attention are turned to the right and into the painting, but your eye stops at the man who looks back at you. These people are motionless in a timeless painting.

VARIETY OR CONTRAST

As in Homer's painting, you have to look carefully to find the ways the artist used contrast in *American Gothic*. Think about what you have read about color, line, and shape in this work. Then, make a list of examples that show variety or contrast in it.

UNIT 4

CORE ACTIVITIES

SELF-PORTRAITS:
American Gothic

Grant Wood's portrait shows the Iowa couple in harmony with their environment. Everything in the painting says something about them—their character, values, tastes, and accomplishments. You will now do a portrait of yourself in an environment that reflects your character and tastes. This will be a strong statement about your values and beliefs.

Begin by writing a short personal profile of you. Then look through photos of yourself. Select one that you feel expresses the qualities you wrote about in your profile. Finally, select an environment that also reflects the values of your profile.

To complete your self-portrait, combine your portrait and the selected background to make a statement about yourself. Give your portrait a title using **"American"** as the first word.

Remember you are to photograph buildings of character; look for details. Student art.

SOCIAL COMMENT:
Photography/Drawing

Grant Wood photographed his Gothic house before he painted it. He had captured something special. Take a series of photographs of buildings with "character" in your community. Look for buildings with unusual details such as Gothic windows. These details can serve as a theme.

On a separate piece of paper, prepare a series of sketches of buildings. Using these sketches, make a compositional drawing. Repeat the shapes as Wood did in the sloping shoulders of his farmer and slanted gables of the house. Do the styles of the buildings in your photos suggest anything about the people who inhabit them or about your community?

THE LAND:
Stylizing a Landscape

Grant Wood stylized natural settings and landscapes. Select a picture of a landscape from a book, magazine, or personal photograph. Analyze the landscape you choose and identify the main repeating shapes. Using *American Gothic, Woman with Plant, Fall Ploughing*, and *Young Corn* as examples, reduce the landscape picture to a composition of geometric figures in the style of Grant Wood. Use colors that reflect the seasons and natural tone of the landscape.

SOCIAL COMMENT:PORTRAITURE
Stylizing the Portrait

In Grant Wood's pencil sketch for *American Gothic*, the angle of the gable repeats in the sloping shoulders of the couple. In this activity you will stylize a portrait by relating your subject to the background as part of a design.

Thomas Eakins, *Max Schmitt in a Single Scull* shows how the artist uses repetition of shape for effect. To suggest the rower's great strength, Eakins repeats the arch of the railroad bridge in the curve of the man's back.

Ingres' *Mlle. Riviere* (1805) is a portrait of a beautiful young woman. Here the artist does not repeat shapes but suggests the shape of a swan in the painting of the woman. She has a swan-like neck, and the swans down stole folds over her arms in the shape of a swan's wings. No swans are swimming on the river, but they are suggested in the shape of Mlle. Riviere (Miss River).

First make a series of pencil sketches of a favorite person or couple in a specific background. Select the best sketch and develop it into a collage. Before doing this activity, look at the artworks on pages 187, 188, 189. Study the portraits and the captions and notice how each artist made his portrait part of a larger design.

STRUCTURAL COMPOSITION:
Variations On a Gothic Arch

American Gothic is a "humorous play of gothic shapes repeating in people, objects, and landscapes." (p. 162) In this lesson you will select one single component (ie. gothic arch) and design a composition using that component repeatedly.

SOCIAL COMMENT—GENRE:
Dreamscapes

Wood's landscapes are described as "rolling hills" that "glide off into distance" (p. 175), and "earthly paradise made by man and his plough." In this activity you will examine the "dreamy corners of nature" by painting an environment of harmony and completeness, something one might see in a dream. All of the components of the painting should promote tensionless harmony, a Utopia of sorts. What kind of landscape might that be?

Alice Liddel was the inspiration for Lewis Carroll's *Alice in Wonderland*. Carroll's photograph suggests how she might have listened to his stories, seated in an uncomfortable chair. The diagonal line of the chair repeats in the position of her body. The design is completed by the lines in her dress.

THE ARTIST SPEAKS ON THE PROBLEM OF LIKENESS

Earlier in the study of *American Gothic*, the question was raised about likeness in a portrait. For some artists likeness is most important—something like a mirror. Others only use likeness to reveal character; still others use the model to tell something about everyone, including the artist. (Most great portraits include all three.)

There is no one or simple answer to this problem of the ages. Since earliest times artists have been making images of people. In ancient Egypt, portraits of kings were part of their immortality. These were supposed to be so lifelike that there would be no mistaken identity in the next world. Looking at these exquisite works today, we can only wonder whether the artists were seeking human likeness or creating beauty.

Thousands of years later, we no longer share the beliefs of the ancient Egyptians, but have feelings about the human image changed? Does a picture have life? If you have any doubts, think of a parent holding a photograph of a child, or our feelings for photographs of loved ones no longer alive. Although only images of people, these photographs are treated with love and respect, as if they were alive.

Figure 125. The coffin of an Egyptian pharoah who probably ruled around 1350 B.C.

Times change and styles change. Each civilization has had its own purpose for portrait painting. But the problem for the artist remains the same: How do I give life to a human image? The artist can find it anywhere; in the face, character, work. Different artists have seen the world in very different ways. There is no one answer to why or how artists make portraits. (Except perhaps that artists have to support themselves!)

WEEPING WOMAN (Pablo Picasso (1881 – 1973)

In an interview, Pablo Picasso was asked about the importance he gave to likeness in portraits. His reply was, "None." "It is not important. The work can be beautiful even if it does not have likeness. What is a face really? Its own photo? Its make up? Or is it a face as painted by such and such painter? Is it that which is in front? Inside? Behind? Doesn't everyone look at himself in a particular way?"

Think about Picasso's statement and look closely at his portrait of the *Weeping Woman, 1937*. Could it possibly resemble anyone? This is a face made from the shapes of broken glass with the characteristic jagged edges, and from colors that clash like flashing lights. Nothing, at first glance, is where it should be. The eyes are out of their sockets—and in this art they are placed in other parts of the face. Are the eyes little "shipwrecked boats" or are they polished diamonds? Look again. What we see is not the portrait of a woman, but what happens to her face when she weeps. There is pain and tears; there is weeping in every

Figure 126. Pablo Picasso's *Weeping Woman, 1937*.

part of the face, while each color tries to scream louder than the others.

Why all this weeping? The reason for her weeping is in part of the title. In 1937, Spain, Picasso's native land, was in the grip of a savage civil war. In the portrait, the woman is Spain, a country torn apart.

Since this painting is considered a masterpiece, what about likeness?

On the following pages we will use Picasso's statement as a guide to three of the world's most famous portraits. Before reading the analysis, look closely at each painting. Decide first if the portrait might have resembled the model. Does it make any difference? Then think about what the artist did to reveal what he alone saw and felt.

MONA LISA   (Leonardo da Vinci 1452 – 1519)

"Every portion of a body and every smaller detail must be given its importance for the exact rendering of light and shadow." (See Figure 127)

The mystery and fascination of the *Mona Lisa* has challenged every generation. The woman is smiling, but what kind of smile is it? No one agrees because Leonardo played a visual trick. A smile can be read in the eyes and the lips. Notice how he put the corners of her eyes and lips in deep shadow, making her smile almost impossible to read. In the mouth and the eyes Leonardo does not record the light and shadow exactly, but uses them for his own mysterious purposes. In the background the two sides of the landscape do not match. The woman seems taller from the left side than on the right, so depending on the angle, she appears differently.

We know some things about the woman and the artist. Mona Lisa was actually an unhappy person. In order to lift her spirits (and smile) when she posed, Leonardo often brought in musicians to play. During his lifetime, Leonardo treasured the work and refused to part with it. Many critics believed he loved the woman (and the portrait).

There is something about the *Mona Lisa* that no book or reproduction can show. When you stand in front of the actual painting, you can see a thin veil of paint between her and you. The veil adds to the mystery. Is she smiling at us, or is it a secret smile for herself alone? Is she laughing at us? We do not know and we cannot go past the veil for the answer. Although everyone can see different things in her

Figure 127. *La Gioconda*, **popularly known as the** *Mona Lisa*, **by Leonardo da Vinci (around 1506).**

face, all agree she is smiling. Leonardo gave to this unhappy person the one quality she most often lacked in life—a smile.

THE BLUE BOY (Thomas Gainsborough 1727 – 1788)

According to the artist Thomas Gainsborough, the true beauty of a portrait was in its likeness to the sitter. "Likeness," he once said, "is the first rule of the painter." His masterpiece, *The Blue Boy*, shows that Gainsborough did not practice what he preached.

The boy in the picture could only have existed in his imagination. Everything is exaggerated: the posture, the perfect noble face, and especially the clothes—that kind of dress had not been worn in England for well over a hundred years. At the first exhibit of *The Blue Boy*, no one knew or recognized the boy. It did not matter, for what people saw was the color blue used in a way no artist had ever done before. At the very center of the painting a blast of blue-white light—a warm, glowing blue—reflects its light in the

Figure 128. *The Blue Boy* by Thomas Gainsborough. (1780)

folds and lace of the silk costume. The painting dazzled and confused the world. Gainsborough, who had always insisted on likeness, had painted a mystery person. Gainsborough who had always objected to fancy dress because "it took away from the likeness of the model," had painted a boy dressed in sumptuous finery. What did it mean?

We now know a little bit more about the mystery of *The Blue Boy*. Sometime in 1779 the artist was asked to do a portrait of the son of a wealthy hardware dealer. About that same time, Gainsborough's chief rival, the artist Sir Joshua Reynolds, had written about the color blue. He claimed it was not possible to make blue the dominant color of a picture. Reynolds insisted on the warm mellow colors (yellows, reds, or yellow-whites) for masses of light in a picture. He used blues, grays, or greens to support and set off the warm colors. Legend has it the artists quarreled over the matter. Accordingly, Gainsborough did *The Blue Boy* to prove his point. But did he? Perhaps Reynolds was thinking of a cold blue and Gainsborough of a warm blue. Whatever the case, the blue-white light of *The Boy Blue* remains one of the great achievements in art.

So what about the likeness? Then, no one knew the boy; today no one cares. But why did the artist paint *The Blue Boy* if it went against all his beliefs? Again, there is no simple answer, except what you can find in the portrait.

THE FAMILY OF CHARLES IV (Francisco Goya 1746–1828)

Francisco Goya said, "Painting selects what is suitable for its purpose. It brings together qualities from different people and concentrates them on one single *fantastic being*. The creator is no mere copyist but acquires the title of inventor."

In 1798, the Spanish artist Francisco Goya received a commission for a group portrait of the royal family of Spain—the family of King Charles IV. Paintings of kings have their own place in the history of portrait painting. These works, known as "regal portraits," show royalty as human monuments. Two good examples of the regal portrait are those of Henry VIII of England by Hans Holbein and Louis XIV of France by Hyacinthe Rigaud.

In these regal portraits the artists gave to the royal sitters the majesty and glory of their position. Dressed in all their finery, these figures are what they are supposed to be— kings. Larger than life, with a divine right of kingship, their

Figure 129. *The Family of Charles IV*, Francisco Goya (1800).

Figure 130. *King Henry VIII* by Hans Holbein, the Younger, painted around 1536.

Figure 131. *King Louis XIV of France* by Hyacinthe Rigaud depicts the majesty of the French king.

portraits dominated the artists' canvases in the same way they ruled the land. This type of picture is probably what Charles IV had in mind; but it is not what he got from Francisco Goya.

These people are not regal. They are monsters. A famous French writer described them as "the country baker and his wife after they won the lottery." But the writer was not being fair to bakers. What he meant, of course, was the way the artist put fancy clothes on crude, vulgar people. Goya had taken honor out of a king's position and replaced it with contempt. Unlike every court painter before him, instead of paying homage, Goya was brutal, and even worse, honest in his portrayal of royalty.

Without mercy, he chose not to protect those highborn people from their inner selves. For what do we have here? According to one writer, "a collection of ghosts!"— frightened children, a bloated vulture of a king, and a crude, nasty queen.

Goya could have lost his job as court painter, or even his head. That the royal family permitted and even liked this work is amazing. Perhaps it was the fine clothes; or perhaps it was the artist's reference to an earlier glorious portrait of Spanish royalty—*The Maids of Honor* by Diego Velásquez. Look closely at *The Maids of Honor*. How would you compare the two paintings?

The setting for *The Maids of Honor* is the artist's studio. At the left is the artist himself working on a painting. In the

Figure 132. Diego Velásquez's delightful scene of court life, *The Maids of Honor* (1656), contrasts with Goya's unpleasant vision.

center is the Princess Margarita with her friends and maids of honor. Her parents, the king and queen, have just entered the room and we see only their reflection in the mirror. It is a happy scene full of light and majesty.

In Goya's work, the artist is also in his studio, but now he is behind the group. Instead of Velásquez's happy princess, Goya placed the strange-looking queen at the center, causing the light to fall on the fat part of her arm. There is a mirror hidden in Goya's work. Can you find it? That's right, the painting is the mirror. Those people are posing in front of a mirror. Notice how in *The Maids of Honor* the people happily look at each other. In Goya's work they are too busy posing, looking at themselves in the mirror. If the mirror cannot hide the truth, neither will the artist.

This unkingly portrait also revealed a personal truth of the artist: Goya's hatred of this royal family and probably of all royalty.

Goya lived in a time of revolution and change. A few years before, both America and France had gotten rid of kings. In Spain, revolution was in the air and Goya was part of it. This work was a statement of revolution. The portrait brought down the king and humbled the royal family.

In *The Family of Charles IV*, Goya invented a series of *fantastic beings*. Like the queen in *Snow White and the Seven Dwarfs*, the family spoke to the mirror and expected flattery. The Spanish master gave them the bitter truth.

FORMS OF EXPRESSION

The Artist in the Community

The artist, through images, challenges time. Through such visual forms as painting, sculpture, prints, drawings, photographs, and crafts, the artist captures a moment and freezes it in time. Perhaps no image is more powerful than that of a portrait, whether it be of one person or several. A portrait can tell us not only about the person or persons portrayed but about the period and culture in which it was produced. It can tell as well about the artist and, often, through our interpretations, about ourselves.

LOOKING AT PEOPLE
THROUGH PAINTING

Mary Stevenson Cassatt was born in Allegheny City, Pennsylvania, in 1845. She was raised in a comfortable environment and aroused the disapproval of her family when she decided to become a serious artist. Nevertheless, she settled in Paris, France, where she devoted her life to her work. She is best known for her paintings of mothers and children.

**Figure 133. Mary Cassatt's
Emmie and Her Child depicts
a scene of warmth and
harmony.**

Look at Cassatt's painting *Emmie and Her Child*. The
mother and child are tenderly unified through both the
placement and gestures of the hands, as well as the heads.
The mother's hands securely hold the child to her, while the
child reassuringly touches the mother's face and hand. Even
the mother's skirt forms a strong broad base at the bottom of
the painting to add to the sense of security and contentment.
The harmonious colors and the broad brushstrokes also
support the focus of this painting, which is the mother-child
relationship.

The Self-Portraits of Rembrandt (1606 – 1669)

The self-portraits of Rembrandt van Rijn invite us to look at the artist as he looked at himself. Self-portraits receive no commissions—the artist is free to paint whatever he chooses to express about himself. Study two of Rembrandt's self-portraits (Figures 134 A and B).

In the first painting the artist was twenty-three years old. It shows the young artist on the verge of success. The look is self-assured; light falls on the zig-zag of the eyebrows, the cocky nose, and the slight bulge of the mouth. Rembrandt used no props and revealed himself through the play of light on his face.

The second portrait is Rembrandt at the age of fifty. Look closely and compare these two works. Between these two works (1629 and 1656) Rembrandt had gone through much suffering. The young man of the first self-portrait was famous, wealthy, and happily married. But the fates were not so kind. His beloved wife, Saskia, and most of his children had, by this time, died. His spendthrift ways caused him financial ruin. Here, in this masterpiece, we see him at fifty. The grieving eyes peer out at the world in mystery and pain; his expression reveals his anguish. The puffy face reflects the red of the lips and his painter's coat. That coat tells much of Rembrandt's commitment to his art.

Figure 134A. *Self-Portrait* by Rembrandt at age 23. (1629)

Figure 134B. *Self-Portrait* by Rembrandt at age 50. (1656)

Figure 135. A young boy's calm is reflected by the landscape in Peter Hurd's *Nito in Springtime*.

Two examples of more traditional portraits are *Nito in Springtime* and *Don Pablo*. These are both by the American artist Peter Hurd. In each picture the landscape adds to the mood of the subject.

Nito in Springtime is a tempera painting. Tempera is a medium made by mixing ground-up pigment with a binding agent and diluting it with water. The binder most often used is egg yolk or egg yolk and white together. Tempera painting requires special handling because it dries so quickly that retouching is almost impossible. Also, the colors dry lighter than they appear when applied. Many artists today still use tempera because of its effect: tempera gives a smooth, fine finish. The brushstrokes are almost impossible to see.

Hurd portrays the boy, Nito, with delicacy. The light and shadow on his face are soft, as is the landscape behind him. The title of the portrait is a play on words. Nito is standing outdoors in the springtime and, as a young boy, he is in the springtime of his life. He is one with the land, full of promise. His face, like a spring flower, is turned to the light. Water, a symbol of nourishment, flows through the landscape and around the boy. *Nito in Springtime* conveys a sense of fresh growth.

By contrast, Hurd's watercolor *Don Pablo* is stark. The man's face and shirt, the hills, and the sky are almost monumental in form. Instead of a wide landscape as that in *Nito in Springtime*, we see a tightly cropped landscape in which there is not much room for growth. Don Pablo's face is already half in dark shadow. He appears thoughtful and resigned. Perhaps he remembers a time when, like Nito, he was filled with a sense of growing, of the dreams and possibilities of the future.

The shadows in *Don Pablo* suggest that the time is late in the day. This painting might have been called *Don Pablo in Autumn*. Why?

Our faces can tell so much about what we are feeling that sometimes, when we do not want someone to know what is truly on our minds, we disguise our feelings. We smile when we are not happy. We look tough when really we are shy and afraid of a new situation. We act friendly to hide that we do

Figure 136. Hurd's *Don Pablo* is of a more somber mood.

not really feel that way toward another person. We could say that when we disguise our feelings in such a way, we are "wearing a mask."

Peter and the Wolf is by the American artist Ben Shahn (1898-1969). The painting shows two boys wearing masks. Ben Shahn was a sensitive observer of people. He liked to tell stories, and for the storyteller, every detail is of interest.

In *Peter and the Wolf*, Shahn gives us clues as to why the boys might be wearing masks. We can see that the boys' hands are in their pockets, their shoulders are leaning back and their stomachs forward, and their feet seem to be moving very slowly as if hesitant. In fact, the boys appear, from the masks down, to be shyly approaching one another. Their shoulders are not squared off and confident. The boys are not extending their hands in greeting. They are, it seems, deciding. What might they be waiting for? When will one or both choose to remove the mask? Have you ever masked

Figure 137. In *Peter and the Wolf,* Ben Shahn observes how people sometimes disguise their feelings when meeting for the first time.

Figure 138. *Self-Portrait Among the Churchgoers* by Ben Shahn (1939).

your feelings when you met someone for the first time, or were in a new situation?

Shahn was a realistic artist. Although he was an imaginative painter, he insisted on accuracy in his pictures. He said: "There's a difference in the way a twelve-dollar coat wrinkles from the way a seventy-five dollar coat wrinkles, and that has to be right."

If Shahn included automobiles in his picture, they would have to be exactly the kind their owners could afford. When he was working on a painting that had rubble in it, he brought gravel in from his driveway in order to study it. "You cannot invent the shape of a stone," he explained.

Shahn often developed his paintings from photographs he had taken. Because he wished his subjects to remain unaware that he was photographing them, he sometimes used a device known as the right-angle viewfinder. This enabled him to appear to be looking through his camera in a direction at a right angle to the unsuspecting subjects.

In *Self-Portrait Among the Churchgoers*, Shahn painted himself peering through his camera, out of the very scene which he is in fact recording. He seems to be an unimportant figure off in the left margin of the painting. The churchgoers go about their business, unaware that they are the focus of a

Figure 139. Judith Leyster's *Self-Portrait* portrays the artist in direct contact with the viewer.

picture. Shahn's self-portrait tells us little about the artist himself—only that as an artist he is an observer of people and the community. Still, Shahn's portrait may be telling us something about himself. Think about his camera. In what way it it like the boys' masks in *Peter and the Wolf*?

Judith Leyster's *Self-Portrait* looks directly at us. She doesn't hide behind a mask or a right-angle viewfinder. Her self-portrait, like the figure compositions in which she specialized, is painted in a lively and loose style.

Leyster was born and lived in Holland during the seventeenth century. She was a pupil of the painter Frans Hals, who influenced her work. Judith Leyster enjoyed wide acclaim during her lifetime and was honored by her native city of Haarlem. Although the pose and costume appear somewhat stiff and uncomfortable, her face as she works is relaxed and engaging. This painting is really a double portrait because it shows the artist working on a portrait of a musician. Both figures in this portrait within a portrait seem to be saying, "Hi! Join us, won't you?"

Compare Judith Leyster's *Self-Portrait* with Adelaide Labille-Guiard's *Portrait of the Artist with Two Pupils*. Labille-Guiard lived and painted in France during the eighteenth century. Her greatest gifts lay in her portraits, which were painted with strength and solid form. In fact, some critics even doubted that she painted her own pictures, believing that a woman could not have created them.

Adelaide Labille-Guiard was an independent woman who, though she was of noble birth and thus was in danger of her life, remained in Paris after the French Revolution (1789-1799) and taught young women who wished to become artists. She challenged the rule that only men could be professors at the art academies. In *Portrait of the Artist with Two Pupils*, she portrays herself not only as a painter but as a teacher. (See Figure 140)

Of particular interest in this painting are the two pupils. One is watching the teacher demonstrate techniques of painting. The other is watching the painter at work on the portrait. Which is which? The directions of the gazes of the young women underscore the portrait's statement that Adelaide Labille-Guiard is both artist and teacher. The expressions on the students' faces indicate admiration and enthusiasm. Labille-Guiard appears comfortable, self-confident, and kindly.

The teacher and two pupils are joined together through their love of art. Their figures form a triangle. The three heads are at the apex. Their full skirts are at the bottom, pointing toward (notice the artist's toe) the strong diagonal of the large canvas. We are looking at a powerful comment about women and art—each forcefully represented. There is yet another important triangle in the picture. Can you find it?

Within the large triangle made up of the three women is a smaller one. To define it, begin with the hair of the pupil farther back. Continue along the shoulder of the pupil next to her, stopping at the hand about her waist. Now follow the left forearm of the pupil closer to the viewer and continue along the forearm of the teacher. Follow the brush in the right hand of the teacher, which points back to the pupil we

Figure 140. In *Portrait of the Artist with Two Pupils,* (1792) Adelaide Labille-Guiard shows us the artist as both subject and teacher.

Figure 141. Triangular designs create a strong sense of unity in Labille-Guiard's painting.

began with. This triangle, like the larger one, is directed toward the painting by the palette and the brushes held in the artist's left hand. There is still another triangle to be found by connecting the eyes of the three women. The women—teacher and pupils—are united, and their focus is art.

Labille-Guiard chose to portray herself as an artist and teacher. That is, she wished to be seen for the things she did. Many portraits show people engaged in their daily routines. This is a way of telling us more about a person than might be possible by just presenting a face and torso.

Children's Doctor is a tempera painting by the American artist Andrew Wyeth. It shows two sides of a physician—Dr. Margaret Handy—front and back. As you can see, a person's back can project a strong statement. Although we see Dr. Handy in the foreground presented in a classic head-and-shoulders portrait, we see her at the same time walking away to make her rounds of visits to the sick. It is almost as if to say that she is too busy to sit very long for a portrait. Her patients are waiting, and she must be off.

The doctor's face, with hand raised to cheek, appears thoughtful and pleasant. Her expression indicates that even as she sits for the portrait, her mind is on other things. The

Figure 142. *Children's Doctor* **by Andrew Wyeth.**

squared-off shape of her back suggests solidity and responsibility. She is a woman in whom many parents and children have placed their trust.

In reality Dr. Handy was a woman of strong determination. She shocked her mother by choosing a career in medicine and was one of the first women to graduate from Johns Hopkins Medical School. She took care of Andrew Wyeth's children as well as those of many of his friends. Wyeth's portrait *Children's Doctor* shows both his fondness and respect for her.

LOOKING AT PEOPLE THROUGH SCULPTURE

Representations of parent and child occur throughout the ages and across all cultures. Almost three thousand years ago, a Mexican artist of the Tlatilco culture created the ceramic *Maternity Figure*. The mother appears to look at us protectingly as her baby snuggles contentedly in her lap.

Figure 143. *Maternity Figure* by unknown Mexican artist.

Figure 144A. These figures from Northwest Mexico show different attitudes that parents have toward their children.

Parents and Children were made by artists from the Colima culture in northwestern Mexico almost one thousand years later. These ceramic figures depict several tribal women and a man holding their children. The mothers are more comfortable than the father, who holds his child awkwardly as though about to hand it over to someone else. Note the variety of ways, all affectionate, that Parents and Children are represented.

The ancient people of Colima lived in a gentle and peaceful society and were a cheerful lot. We find clear evidence of this in their freehand modeled-clay figures, which are outstanding both for their variety and character. How much personality comes across through these simple clay shapes!

Queen and Hairdresser is a sunk relief sculpture from Egypt dating back to about 2050 B.C. In raised relief the background is cut away and the figure is left standing. In sunk relief the figure is "sunk" into the background, which is left untouched. In the brilliant light of Egypt, sunk relief had a more dramatic effect than raised relief.

Figure 144B. An ancient carving of a child at play (Mexico).

Figure 145. This fragment of an Egyptian carving from the tomb of an Egyptian queen is about 4000 years old.

Queen and Hairdresser is a fragment. It came from the underground tomb chamber of Queen Neferu at Thebes. In the sculpture the queen is attended by her hairdresser, who is attaching an artificial braid. Just in front of the braid being attached is another lock which is pinned up out of the way until the new braid is in place. Notice that the profiles of both the queen and her hairdresser are almost identical. That is because they are not meant to represent real individuals. Instead, they represent the female face considered to be the ideal at the time. The women have full lips, a prominent nose with strong nostrils, slanting ears, and dramatic eyes.

Which portrait tells you more about its subject, the Wyeth painting *Children's Doctor* or the *Queen and Hairdresser* sculpture? Or do those works tell you different things?

LOOKING AT PEOPLE THROUGH PHOTOGRAPHY

You have seen how painters and sculptors portrayed people. Now let us look at how photographers capture people's portraits on film.

The photograph *Bicyclists* brings us abruptly face to face with three young men on a country road. The artist, August Sander, traveled around his country, Germany, looking for faces to photograph. His photographs skillfully unveil the private person in the public face. He has brought us up close to the bicyclists by cropping (cutting off) the photograph so that there is very little foreground between them and us. We are almost forced to confront them.

What are these three bicyclists telling us about themselves as they stop to pose for a picture? Is there a leader in the group? Who is he and why do you think he is the leader?

What do you learn from observing the attitudes of the bodies? The positions of the hands? The hats? And, of course, the facial expressions?

These young men are trying to convince us that they are self-assured and persons to be reckoned with. Although they are dressed as grown men, they are trying too hard to look like what they think grown men look like. The expressions on their faces are very similar. As we look at the photograph, the three faces begin to merge into one person.

Figure 146. The three subjects in August Sander's *Bicyclists* confront the viewer.

Do you think each bicyclist would have the same expression on his face if he were traveling alone? Sander has created a tension between the subjects of the photograph and the viewer. The three boys seem to be daring us to take on their group. As viewers we try to separate the boys from the security of their "threeness" so that each stands alone.

The sharp detail in such Sander photographs as *Bicyclists* and *Unemployed* encourages us to approach the subjects with an almost scientific curiosity. Indeed, Sander was seeking to photograph universal "types" of people. Therefore, he never listed the names of his subjects but rather the

Figure 147. By contrast, the subject in Sander's *Unemployed* stands alone looking away from the viewer.

activity or occupation. What "type" of person is the man shown in *Unemployed?* Unlike the cocky youths portrayed in *Bicyclists*, he holds his hat humbly and low before him. He does not stand boldly in the middle of the road but off to the side of the street. He is out of the mainstream, no longer a part of the daily traffic. Compare his posture and facial expression to those of the young men. What differences do you find?

The Art of Imogen Cunningham (1883 – 1976)

When Imogen Cunningham died at the age of ninety-three, she was still working, still taking photographs. Encouraged by her father to develop her talent, she became a portrait photographer at a time when there were few women in the profession.

As a photographer, Imogen developed the art of "breaking through the mask" to portray the real person underneath. While working, she posed questions to her sitters about their lives to get the right expression. Suddenly came the moment of truth—the snap of the shutter reflected the moment of the artist's greatest concentration. The result is now a large collection of unforgettable portraits.

In the 1970s she began a series of portraits of people over ninety years old. The photographs have much to tell about the tragedy and the triumph of the elderly. Take a look at several of Imogen Cunningham's photographs from her remarkable collection.

The first two photographs are of the sculptor John Roeder. His hands tell everything. This man worked in an oil refinery, but said Imogen "he was really an artist." Notice how the strong character is revealed in the lines of his hands and face. The second photograph of the two shows the sculptor standing beside one of his creations. Now the hands, in a fatherly way, gently touch his proud upright child.

Figure 148C is a black woman in a senior-citizens home. Her face reminds us of Miss Jane Pittman. At the home the world has forgotten about her. But she has seen much and has survived. Her face tells us she will continue to survive.

The title of Figure 148D is *The Three Ages of Woman, on Fillmore Street*. In this photograph are childhood innocence, motherhood, and in front an elderly, frail woman—still full of life. The lines on her face and the powerful gaze into the lens dominate her children, as does the background tree

Figure 148A. John Roeder worked in an oil refinery, but was really an artist.

Figure 148B. Here is John with one of his sculptures.

Figure 148A.

Figure 148B.

Figure 148C. She said to me, "When you come here, nobody knows where you are."

Figure 148E.

Figure 148E. My father at 90.
Figure 148F. Michelangelo's *Moses*

Figure 148F.

which dominates its fruits. The title might have been "The Tree of Life" or "The Courage to Live."

Figure 148D is a loving portrait of Imogen Cunningham's father at age 90. He resembles the biblical Moses carved by Michelangelo (Figure 148F).

Another photographer, Brassai, also made a portrait of a painter. In *Picasso, rue de la Boetie* (1937), Brassai shows us the master painter Pablo Picasso in his studio.

The body and the room are in shadows. The lighting focuses attention on the face and those piercing, haunting eyes. Brassai had seen those eyes in many of Picasso's paintings. Study the composition of the photograph.

Your eye travels in a circle from the background clutter of paints and palletes back to the intense face. As relaxed as he is, Picasso was not off guard. Brassai regarded the taking of photograph as an artistic event. He wanted his subjects totally aware of the act.

Brassai began his creative career as a painter and writer. He became interested in photography because he enjoyed wandering about the city at night. He sought a medium which would enable him to fix the images he found to be so interesting. Perhaps some of his writer's sensibilities appear in his photographs. He once said:

"I want my subject to be as fully conscious as possible—fully aware that he is taking part in an artistic event, an act. Do you remember the old cameras that the village photographer used at the turn of the century? Large as an oak tree, with a lens cap the size of a cat's face, and a billowing black hood? All the village came to have marriage and confirmation pictures taken. It was a solemn, almost holy event. You were obliged to sit still; with the old lens cap the exposure was sometimes four minutes. Moreover, you had to hold your breath, sit still, and stare 'at the dickey bird.' The fact that it was ritual did something to the sitter—you can see the souls looking out of their faces more easily than you can in our photographs of today. They were not off guard, but fully cooperative, sharing an act of innocent majesty—'having a picture took.' That is what I still try to hunt for."

Look at one of Brassai's most famous photographs, *Two Hoodlums 1932*. The faces of two young toughs emerge from behind a dark wall. Light catches the defiance in their eyes, mouths, and twisted cloth caps. This is a menacing photograph.

Brassai made photographs at night with a flash bulb if the

Figure 149. Brassai's photograph, *Picasso, rue de la Boetie*.

Figure 150. Brassai snapped the photograph, *Two Hoodlums 1932* in the middle of the night.

Figure 151. *Lady Thepu* **is a portrait of a woman of royalty who lived about 1400 B.C.**

light was too dim. In 1930, this was considered almost impossible, but the results are unforgettable portraits of the human face. Who knows what terrible things these two have done, or are about to do.

As you have seen, a portrait can show many aspects of a person—moods, feelings, work, how others view that person, and so on. A portrait can also be a kind of social comment. It can tell something about the times and society in which it was made. Let us look at two very different such portraits.

One is a painting called *Lady Thepu*. The other is Edward Steichen's photograph *Portrait of a Portraitist*. Both portraits show women dressed in finery. Lady Thepu lived in Egypt about 1400 B.C. Gertrude Käsebier (Steichen's subject) was an American portrait photographer who lived from 1852-1934.

Lady Thepu wears a heavy wig on her head. Her forehead is decorated with a diadem and her neck with a rich collar. She wears a white dress, with a filmy shawl about her shoulders. Lady Thepu is dressed in the style of the great ladies of her time.

Gertrude Käsebier was a career woman in a time when most women didn't work. Steichen has managed to convey both her strength of character and her femininity in his portrait.

Compare the two portraits. Both show mature women. Lady Thepu, however, is represented in an idealized form suggesting the glory of youth. Gertrude Käsebier is not idealized but instead appears thoughtful and sensitive. The two portraits, *Lady Thepu* and *Portrait of a Portraitist* tell us about very different times and very different lives.

Wright Morris is an artist who works with both verbal and visual images. Each two-page spread of his photo-text books is made up of a page of text facing a photograph. In his book *God's Country and My People*, Morris portrayed the Midwest he remembered it as a boy. He says of his work:

> "This recombining of the visual and the verbal, full of my own kind of unpeopled portraits, sought to salvage what I considered threatened, and to hold fast to what was vanishing."

Figure 152. *Portrait of a Portraitist* by Edward Steichen.

Although these photographs show other people, they are also a kind of self-portrait of Wright Morris. They portray the world he comes from and loves deeply. It is in this world that the roots of his identity lie.

Harry's Boy, Will is a portrait within a portrait. We see on the wall above the chair a picture of Will when he was a young boy. Morris tells us in the text what became of the boy in that portrait. Even as we look at Will up there on the wall, we are learning from the text that that boy no longer exists.

Figure 153. Elements of a family drama are contained in *Harry's Boy, Will* by Wright Morris.

Figure 154. *On This Occasion* **is another example of Morris's ability to tell stories through the objects in his photographs.**

The boy Will still lives in the old man's house, but the man Will disagreed with his father and never set foot in the house again.

Harry's Boy, Will is in part a self-portrait of Wright Morris, because it tells us something about the world in which he grew up. Like Will, we imagine, he left home and a room like the one we see to learn new ways.

On This Occasion is a moving portrait/self-portrait. Morris's text tells us that we are looking at a picture of the artist's mother which sits on a dresser in his father's room. As we look at the tiny picture of his mother, his father talks about her in the text. In telling something of Wright's mother, his father tells a great deal about himself as well. In turn, this helps us to learn more about their artist son.

Figure 155.
Morris's *There's Little to See*
demands that the viewer
take a closer look.

Wright's third photograph is called *There's Little To See.*
What is there to see? Only an impression left by someone's
weight on a bed and a pair of shoes. Look again. This time
use all your senses and your imagination. What do you "see"
now? Although the bed is empty, there is the sensation that
it has not been empty long. If you put your hand on the
coverlet, you might still feel the warmth of whoever was just
there. The whole room seems to vibrate with the warmth of
whomever was in it. Who might that person be?

Think about this photograph. What kind of a portrait is
it? How does it differ from Brassai's photograph *Two Hoodlums*? In what way is it similar?

LOOKING AT PEOPLE
THROUGH PRINTS

Many artists are printmakers. A print is a work of art that
can be produced in multiple copies. Some types of prints are

etchings, woodcuts, engravings, silkscreens, and litho-graphs.

Let us look first at a lithograph by the artist Kaethe Kollwitz. This print, *Poverty*, shows a mother and child.

As in the painting *Emmie and Her Child* by Mary Cassatt, the placement of the hands is important to this portrait. The child's hands are drawn together under the sheets. The mother's hands hold her head in grief. Again as in Cassatt's painting, the background is subordinated so that our attention focuses on the mother and child. And Kollwitz's mother and child form a triangle, just as they do in Cassatt's painting.

However, the triangle in *Emmie and Her Child* suggests stability and perhaps contentment. The triangle in *Poverty* suggests despair.

Look at the triangle formed by the mother's head (at the top), arms and elbows (at the sides), and baby in bed (at the base). The weight of the mother (and her sorrow) appears to be concentrated at her elbows. They seem to reach for a base on which to rest. Her physical weight and her hopes as a mother are about to collapse as her child lies dying.

Figure 156. *Poverty*, a lithograph by Kaethe Kollwitz.

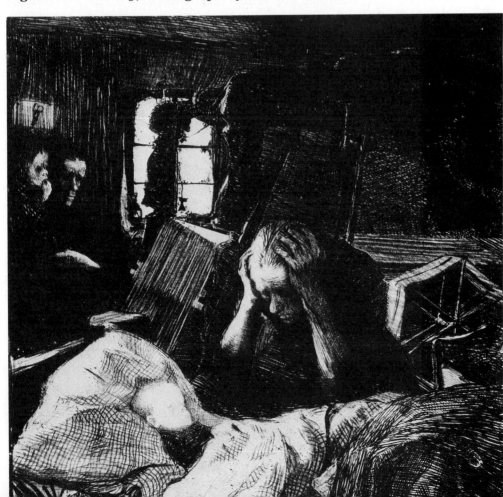

Although Kaethe Kollwitz studied painting and drawing, printmaking was her major interest. She was more interested in line than color, and her drawings were always a means to an end. They were studies for a print. Kollwitz was also attracted to the graphic arts because she believed in making original works widely available at low cost.

Poverty is an example of Kollwitz's interest in social drama, and in the plight of workers and their struggle to improve their position. *Poverty* is one of a series of prints dramatizing the problems of weavers. In the mid-nineteenth century the Industrial Revolution was sweeping through Europe. The invention of power looms meant that weavers who worked by hand were no longer needed. Thus, *Poverty* represents not only the death of a child but the death of a way of life for these hand weavers. Their weaving equipment rests idly in the background of the picture, as do the woman and child to the viewer's left. The artist presents us with a powerful statement regarding the effects of social change.

Artists record their responses to the people and activities in their communities in a variety of ways. One way is through art which shows scenes from everyday life. Remember, for example, how John Sloan in *Backyards, Greenwich Village* (page 73) showed us a scene from everyday life in which children are simply having a good time in the snow. Pieter Brueghel's *Hunters in the Snow*, (page 71) too, shows people involved in the commonplace activities of another time.

Small-scale works of art showing scenes from everyday life are called "genre" art. Italian and Flemish artists began to produce such work back in the fourteenth and fifteenth centuries. It emerged as a distinct art form in the seventeenth century in the work of the Dutch and Flemish masters. In the twentieth century many Impressionists and Post-impressionists took it up. *Genre* is a French word meaning "sort" or "variety."

Look at the three graphic prints by the American artist Edward Hopper. Hopper spent most of his life in New York City. His work portrays everyday scenes of the city, often stressing its lonely mood.

House Tops, Night in the Park and *The Movies,* all show a human presence in a nearly deserted space—train, theater, park. The geometric character of these places is emphasized by harshly revealing light. These everyday scenes have been simplified so that they are emotionally charged and

Figure 157. *House Tops,* an etching by Edward Hopper, is an example of "genre" art.

Figure 158. Hopper's *Night in the Park* depicts the solitude possible even in the city.

appear almost unearthly. The solid forms give a somewhat sculptural sense to all three pictures. Although these prints reflect genre-like subjects, their true meaning goes beyond just an everyday activity.

**Figure 159A.
Edward Hopper's
painting of
The Movies, New York
(1928).**

**Figure 159B.
A study by Hopper
for his painting
The Movies, New York.**

Edward Hopper

Figure 159C. A free-hand sketch/drawing of Hopper's prior to his painting *The Movies, New York.*

The people in each of these prints are faceless. The artist was less concerned with individuals than with the image of people alone with their thoughts. Because we do not see anything particular or unique about the person, we can concentrate on understanding what the figure in each of these settings represents about all people.

In *Night in the Park*, a man reads about the lives and events of other people in the newspaper. He too is alone. The spotlight in all three of these pictures is on a world of other people beyond the central figure—the house tops, the movie screen, the newspaper. The subjects are in deep shadow—physically outside that world but connected to it by their thoughts.

In each example, we are looking, from behind or unobserved, at someone looking at something. In *House Tops* and *The Movies*, although there are two figures, they are not communicating with each other. Each is alone with his thoughts. Perhaps the artist is saying that even when we are in the midst of other people, we are also alone.

The central person in each print is part of society, but

separated from it at the same time. Perhaps that is what makes the pictures so lonely. The woman in *House Tops* is traveling on a public vehicle. She turns to gaze out of the window at the houses passing by. They are evidence of the lives of other people. Perhaps the woman wonders who lives in those houses, or how their lives differ from her own. What do you think she might be seeing out there?

The woman in *The Movies* has her hands folded as though in thought. She stands alone, probably watching from a distance the lives of other people. Others in the theater offer no comfort or sense of companionship. Each woman appears to be alone in her own world.

Edward Hopper is commenting through his work on a relationship between people and society of which he was strongly aware. The works we have looked at are making a social comment. What is that comment? What techniques and compositional devices strengthen the artist's purpose?

LOOKING AT PEOPLE THROUGH DRAWINGS

We have seen in the photographs of Imogen Cunningham (see Figures 148 A and B) how expressive a person's hands can be. Sometimes people's hands can tell us more about them than their faces. In Henry Moore's crayon and water-color drawing *Women Winding Wool*, the hands tell the

Figure 160. *Women Winding Wool*, a 1949 drawing by English artist Henry Moore.

story. The figures of the two women strike us as great, solid forms resting in place like two continents. They are connected by a moving "sea" of wool. They communicate through the tensions created as they move the wool to keep it taut between them. They do not have to talk. We do not have to see their faces to know what they are communicating.

The tension we see in the threads of wool is repeated by a larger theme—the tension between two strong figures, separate and connected at the same time. It is their hands that bring them together. The tension in this picture is further shown by the technique with which it has been recorded. Short, nervous strokes of the crayon create an impression of flowing energy. Winding wool becomes a lively dialogue.

Figure 161. In Yasuo Kuniyoshi's *Girl Thinking*, the viewer learns about the girl by looking at her hands.

In the ink drawing *Girl Thinking*, by Yasuo Kuniyoshi, the hand is important to the mood of contemplation. It is likely that Kuniyoshi meant us to focus on the hand. Our eye is drawn to its white shape which contrasts with the dark areas of the face and hair. Looking more closely at the hand we see that it presses into the lips, showing that they are loose and flexible rather than set. The girl's eyes appear to be gazing into herself as well as out of the picture. Whatever she is thinking about, the girl does not seem to have made up her mind yet. The loose, sketchy brushwork corresponds to her thoughts; she is musing, letting her mind drift.

Earlier in this unit, we looked at two portraits that showed youth and age. Do you recall Peter Hurd's *Nito in*

Figure 162. *Three Studies of the Head of a Young Negro* by French artist Jean Antoine Watteau (eighteenth century).

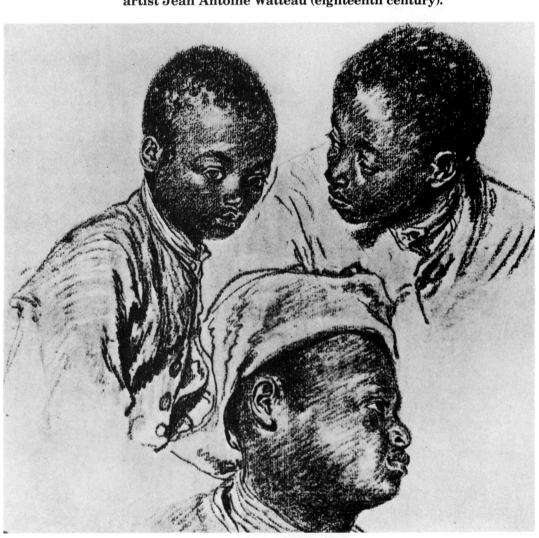

**Figure 163. Albrecht Dürer
drew this work titled
Mother of the Artist (1514).**

Springtime and *Don Pablo?* (Figures 135/136) Now, let's
look at another pair of portraits that show youth and age.
They are Jean Antoine Watteau's *Three Studies of the Head
of a Young Negro* (detail) and Albrecht Dürer's, *Mother of
the Artist*. Both are drawings. The first is executed with
chalk and watercolor; the second illustration is a charcoal
drawing. There is no landscape present in either to help us
with our interpretations. The figures stand alone.

In *Three Studies of the Head of a Young Negro* and *Mother
of the Artist* the eyes are very expressive. The youth's eyes
are open wide, perhaps to show his openness to life. At first
glance the old woman seems tough with no love and affec-
tion. But the left eye, almost out of its socket shows love and
feeling. This woman has experienced much suffering. What
can that mean? What do these portraits by Watteau and
Dürer have in common with *Nito in Springtime* and *Don
Pablo* (pages 206-207)? How are they different?

You have now looked at many different kinds of portraits
in several different mediums. You have seen how artists
portray themselves, other individuals and groups, as well as
society in general. You have seen that with just one portrait
an artist can say a great deal. As in all artwork, the vision of
the portrait artist must communicate itself to us. The artist
must find in the outside world the clues to his or her inside
world.

Look around you. Whom do you see? Who seems to be wearing a mask? Why? Watch the people around you engaged in everyday activities, at school, at home, at the store, on the street. How much do you see? What visual clues do you perceive? Some people and events appear to be one way one minute, another way the next. What is really happening? How can you tell the difference? How good an observer are you? Watch what is going on and see how many surprises you can find.

Summary Questions

1. Name three things that a portrait can tell us.

2. How does Ben Shahn combine imagination and accuracy in his portraits?

3. What is the difference between raised and sunk relief in sculpture?

4. How did photographer Imogen Cunningham think an ideal portrait should be obtained?

5. In what way is Kaethe Kollwitz's lithograph *Poverty* a social commentary?

6. What is a print?

7. What is "genre" art?

8. Give an example of how an artist has used hands to convey character in a drawing.

UNIT
5

ACTIVITIES

1. Know About Art   Being able to recognize and understand terms used in describing certain art forms is an important part of the study of the visual arts. One term that is often used is *portrait*. What does it mean? A portrait is a representation of a person. Sometimes it shows only the face—sometimes the full figure of the subject. The artists you have read about have created portraits of their subjects in different ways.

Look in magazines, travel brochures, museum bulletins, old postcards, and other sources to find examples of portraits. Mount your examples and those of your classmates in a class Portrait Gallery. Discuss the faces, positions of the heads, kinds of clothing, and backgrounds. Do these details tell you something about the person in the portrait? What do they tell you?

2. Self-Portrait   Use yourself as the subject of a portrait. Decide how you want to dress for your portrait. Next look in the mirror. As you do, make a series of sketches of yourself using a light wash, large piece of chalk, or a water marker. Overlap a series of these sketches. You might paint the shapes and spaces as they are created by the overlapping. Add the final details of clothing and background after your composition is blocked in with color.

3. Drawing: Reportage   This drawing activity will test your observation skills. First practice drawing a variety of lines with your pencils, such as thick, soft lines and thin, sharp lines.

One of your classmates will model in a costume. Before beginning to draw, observe. Look at the details of the costume. Look and try to remember every part of the costume and how it fits the student. Close your eyes and try to recall how the different parts of the costume are made. Now look again to see if you remembered correctly.

After the model has left the room, take out your pencils and draw the model and the costume from memory. When the drawing is finished, the model will return and you can compare your drawing with the real costume.

This kind of drawing is called *reportage drawing*. Practicing this skill several times a week will help you develop your observation skills. At first look at and then draw simple objects like a rock, cup, or hat. Look at the object for a few minutes, then put it away and try to draw it accurately. Move from simple to more complex objects as you gain skill.

4. Drawing: Using Frames Make a composing frame. You'll need a 5 x 8-inch index card. Cut a hole approximately 1 x 1 inch in the center. Holding it at arms length, view a landscape or a still life set up in the art room. Move the frame closer to your eye. What happens? Study many "framed" sections of the still life or landscape before you decide on one you wish to draw. A composing frame will help you compose your drawing. As you do more and more drawings, it will become easier to compose without this aid.

**Printmaking.
Student art.**

5. Printmaking: Relief Collograph Look at pictures of landscapes, paintings, or photographs. Can you find in these pictures any shapes that repeat? Do any shapes overlap others? This activity deals with the repetition of shapes found in rural or urban landscapes. The printing material is a relief collograph.

First use a dark magic marker to sketch a landscape on a piece of lightweight cardboard. Think of the shapes you see in the scene. Sketch only the big shapes in the scene being careful to allow for overlapping. You'll add details later. Cut the shapes out of cardboard and glue them down to another sheet of cardboard. Next add the details. If, for example, you are using skyscraper shapes, add windows. Are they all the same size and shape? Are there any decorative elements around the windows? Adding texture and details like power lines, door knobs, light posts, bus stops, or different kinds of trees makes a collograph more interesting.

When you have finished the details, paint your plate with a coat of acrylic polymer, rhoplex, or even white acrylic house paint. This seals the plate, making it easier to print.

To make prints of your plate: Roll water-base ink or thick paint onto the plate with a brayer. Medium pressure should be used to cover the plate with a thin, even coat of ink. Carefully lift the inked plate from the inking area, and place it face up on a clean sheet of paper. Then place another clean sheet of paper over the inked plate. The paper should be large enough to leave a margin of at least an inch on all sides. Quickly rub the covered plate with your fingertips or the heel of your hand. Peel off the paper. Your first print is finished. Hang it up to dry and repeat the printing process until you have five prints. These five prints are your edition.

6. People Collages Grant Wood told you something about the characters in *American Gothic* by dressing them as he did. Create people who tell a story by the kinds of clothes they wear. One way to do this is to make people collages. Obtain a supply of magazines, wallpaper, gift wrapping papers, doilies, and other kinds of interesting papers. On a large sheet of paper, draw an outline figure of a person. Continue by "dressing" the figure. Use the paper supply you have to cut out clothes for the figure. Think carefully about the person you are "dressing." Does this person like fancy, colorful clothes? Or does the person have simple taste? Might the person live on a farm and wear work clothes or does the person work in an office and wear business clothes? Does the person like hats, boots, gloves? What decisions will tell about the person? Cut out clothes for this person and paste them on the outline figure. You might then want to add details to the figure such as facial features. When you are finished you may play a guessing game with classmates. Ask them to guess what kind of person your figure is, based on what the person is wearing.

7. Ceramics/Pottery In this activity you will use a rolled out slab of clay to construct a container. It is helpful to use two smooth dowels as tracks or supports in rolling out the slabs of clay.

Begin by placing a damp cloth on the table. Then put a ball of the clay between the dowels. Using a rolling pin long enough to rest on each dowel, roll the clay to an even thickness. It may be necessary to place a damp cloth over the top to keep the clay from sticking to the rolling pin. Cut a rectangle of clay that will be the base. Roll out and cut another slab that will be long enough to go around the top of the base. Cut the long edges vertically and the end edges on a diagonal. Stand the rectangle on its side on the base slab and gently bend so that it surrounds the slab. Crosshatch

SPECIAL ACTIVITY: An Artist Speaks About His Work

The Slab Pot

Many forms can be made using the slab clay method; the slab pot is only one. The slab can be pounded with the heel of the hand or rolled to the desired thickness with the common kitchen rolling pin (*Figure 164A*). To prevent the clay from sticking, it should be rolled out on a piece of canvas. This allows for easy transfer. A dry plaster slab or grog dusted on a table top will serve the same purpose. If the proposed form is rather flat, the clay pieces must be leather hard before assembly begins. The joints should be scored and covered with clay slip. Since flat, horizontal sections tend to sag during construction and in firing, it is advisable to insert clay partition walls. These must have cut-out openings to allow for drying.

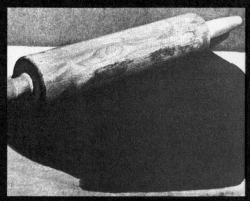

Figure 164A. Rolling out the clay slab.

Figure 164B. Pinching together the edges of the clay slab.

where the edges meet to secure the slab. That is the basic construction process. Start fairly small. With practice you can make much larger pots with the slab method.

Figure 164D. A carved slab is added to form the top of the pot.

Figure 164C. The upper edge of the pinched clay slab is scored with a tool.

Figure 164E. Spouts and legs can be thrown or pinched separately.

Figure 164F. Decorative lines are incised in the finished piece.

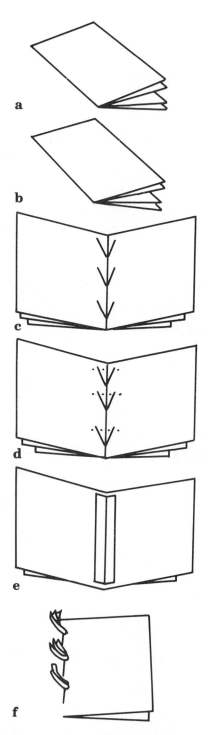

Figure 165. Bookmaking.

8. Bookmaking With this method of bookbinding, no sewing or weaving is needed. The book is held together by folds.

First decide if your book will have a vertical or a horizontal format. What size do you want the pages to be? Stack the pages together with a cover. The cover should be made of a contrasting color and should be slightly larger than the text on all sides. Fold in half (*a*). Cut three slits at an angle into the folded book (*b*). Open the book out flat (*c*). Push the V-shaped tabs now formed outward (*d*) and flatten them back. While the book is still opened flat, paste a strip of paper on the inside fold to cover the triangular holes in the middle (*e*).

An interesting effect is achieved when the strip is a different color than the cover. You might use a patterned piece of wrapping paper for this strip. Carefully refold the book in half. The tabs will fan out. Work them with your fingers until flat and curling upward (*f*). By cutting into the spine at different angles you can get different effects.

9. Photography: Three-Dimensional Pop-up
In some compositions, images seem to project out from the picture toward the viewer. Experiment with three-dimensional

Pop-up. Student art.

effects in photographs. Find a photo that you can cut up. Which elements in this photograph would you like to stand out? Use exacto knives or single-edged razor blades to carefully cut around the edge of the elements you have chosen. Then cut pieces of foam rubber, corrugated or foam board the same size as the photo cutout or cutouts. Glue the photo to a piece of paper. Glue each photo cutout to a piece of foam rubber and glue the foam rubber where the photo cutout belongs in the photograph. The foam rubber will project the element out of the picture and create a three-dimensional effect.

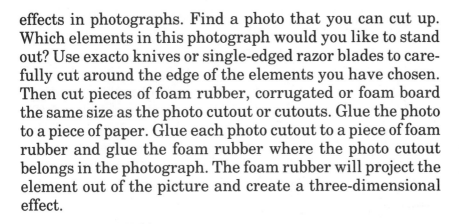

10. Photograph: Pinhole Camera   The figures in Grant Wood's *American Gothic* look as if they are posing for a photographer. In the early days of photography, emulsions were slow (not as sensitive to light) and the shutter had to stay open for a long time. People had to pose very still for a photographic portrait to be made. Lenses also were not as powerful in earlier cameras.

The pinhole camera you will make will also require the photographic subject to remain very still during the photographing process.

For a pinhole camera you will need a shoe box, or an oatmeal box, or a cigar box. Paint the inside of the box flat black. Use a fine sewing needle to poke a pinhole in a piece of aluminum foil. (A more durable and uniformly round pinhole can be made by *almost* piercing a heavier pie tin foil with a needle and then sanding it on the reverse side until a hole appears.) Cut a small opening (1 x 1 inch) in the box and tape the foil in with the pinhole in the middle of the opening. This serves as your lens and aperture. For your light sensitive emulsion, tape photographic paper or sheet film opposite the pinhole, inside the box while you are in a darkroom or closet. Then use black tape to make sure the box is light tight at the seams.

To take a picture, go outdoors. Find a subject and focus the camera on it. Exposure time varies with time of day and emulsion type. It will be a few seconds for film and about ten minutes for paper. Devise a shutter or cover for the pinhole which can be held in place after the exposure.

11. Photography: The Portrait   Set up and take a photographic portrait. Plan this portrait to show as much as possible about the subject. For example, what is the subjects's special interest? Is the person gentle, active, serious? What is a typical body language of your subject? Create a portrait reflecting the individuality and capturing the personality of your subject. Move your model around to see the face in different angles. Experiment with different backgrounds such as a landscape, windows, sky. A background can also tell about a person. Or you might choose a simple background such as white cloth or cardboard covered with foil to fill in deep shadows. Try taking outdoor and indoor exposures. Expose at least one roll of film on your portrait subject. Examine your portrait prints. Which portrait do you like best? Why? Which portrait does your subject like best? Why?

12. Photography: Portraits Without Faces Many painted and photographic portraits have a face as the center of interest. But in this assignment no faces will be visible. Photograph subjects who are wearing masks, helmets, umbrellas, or hats. Be sure that you don't photograph the person's face or reveal his or her identity.

This assignment can also be accomplished by lighting the subject from behind or in silhouette. Set up and take an

**Student art.
Portrait Without Face.**

interesting portrait without relying on the face to create the interest for the composition.

13. Paper Quilting The people in Grant Wood's painting were hard working and thrifty, saving many things to be used over and over again. If a dress was made, all the scraps were saved and made into a bright, warm quilt. In these quilts, one design motif was repeated many times until the desired size was achieved.

Make your own quilt design with scraps of construction paper and pieces of wallpaper. Cut these scraps into circles, squares, and triangles. Arrange them on a piece of construction paper to form a motif that could be used for a quilt or quilted pillow. When you have a balanced and pleasing design, glue the pieces in place.

THE ROLE OF THE ARTIST IN SOCIETY

What was Grant Wood's role as an artist in the town where he lived? Was it the same as other people's? Or does the artist have a role that goes beyond? In the long history of art, the role of the artist has changed as the community evolved. These changes reflected the differing needs of the community for artists, as well as the artists' responses to those needs.

Artists have not always been called by that word. In prehistoric cave communities and in tribal societies, there was no word for art. The person who painted visual images was the "shaman," a magician-priest. He created magical images which helped to capture the bison, perhaps, or to predict the future.

Later, in the ancient civilizations of Egypt, Sumeria, Greece, and Rome, and throughout the Middle Ages up to the time of Colonial America, the person who painted images and decorations on walls was called an *artisan*. An artisan was part of the working class, and in some cultures was also a slave. Craftspeople were also of this class. They had great skill in using their hands and creating illusions. They worked in the dirt of the street or the dust of the cathedral, or in a public building as it was being constructed. There was no mystery to their work. They painted what they were told to paint by the master builder or high

Figure 166. The shaman or magician-priest.

priest. Artisans and craftspeople belonged to guilds, as did
stonemasons and other laborers.

The term *artist* was saved for poets, writers, and musicians. These people used their minds to create ideas and
entertainments, not just their hands.

What happened to change all that? Three geniuses—
Leonardo da Vinci, Michelangelo, and Raphael—were
responsible. These artists all lived in the 1400s and 1500s.
They were three of the greatest artists of the period known
as the Renaissance. The Renaissance was a time of new
ideas and great learning. It takes its name from the French
word meaning "rebirth."

During the Renaissance artists made important studies of
the human body, created their own interpretations of myths
and religion, discovered rules for perspective, and helped
develop the principles of design we have been studying in
this book.

Before the Renaissance, the role of the artisan had been to
decorate public buildings, temples, churches, and the homes
of the wealthy. They often painted scenes from mythology

and religious history. Artisans were sometimes asked to paint scenes of conquests for kings and rulers who wanted to impress the world with their authority and power. In the American colonies, artisans decorated carriages and furniture. They also painted picture signs for taverns, shops, and businesses so that uneducated people could read them.

The main role of the artist in Roman Catholic countries such as Italy and Spain was to glorify the Church and bring spiritual inspiration to the people. In countries such as France and England, the main role of the court painter was to paint royalty. In France artisans decorated palaces with scenes of happy people playing games and enjoying themselves.

By the 1700s the Industrial Revolution had begun in England. It spread to other countries in the 1800s. For artists, the Industrial Revolution meant some important changes in the materials they used. Artists could now paint on canvases woven in factories. They could use processed pigments and oils and varnishes which allowed them to work in studios in their homes. Fewer and fewer artists worked on the walls of public buildings.

Some artists became businesspeople. Some became gallery owners who sold their own work and that of other painters. Still, many artists were unable to sell their work and so were very poor. We're all familiar with the image of the hungry, but free-spirited artist working at an easel in an attic.

Because of this freedom to choose their own subject matter and to live and think as they wished, artists were also free to make statements about the world around them. Sometimes they made fun of human frailties and follies. Sometimes they spoke out against cruelty and war. They could also bring power to public events. They could make paintings that moved people for various causes. Their paintings could expose social injustice, and perhaps inspire change.

In the twentieth century, the artist is also the illustrator, the industrial designer, or the commercial artist who designs packaging and advertising. The work of the illustrator usually accompanies something else—poems, stories, novels, textbooks, catalogs, advertisements, and posters. At one time, illustrations were considered a minor art. Today, however, illustrations, posters, advertisements, and books all find places in art museums and galleries.

Now what was Grant Wood's role in his community? He

Figure 167. A commercial artist.

was a keen observer of people and his national heritage. In *American Gothic* he poked fun at our rigidities and resistance to anything new or different. In *Victorian Survival* he noted how we hold on to the past in spite of change and "progress." In *The Appraisal*, he told a story of conflict between people of the farm and of the city and between two ways of life.

In *Fall Ploughing,* however, Wood glorifies rather than ridicules. He shows us the land, the real American landscape, the heartland. He exults in the sunshine in the field, the neat rows of haystacks, the furrows of plowed fields. The rows lead to the real heart of Grant Wood's beliefs. The farm with its farmhouse, barns, and windmill perches there on the edge of a hill, like a cathedral in a medieval landscape. Grant Wood's role in the community, in the nation, and in the world, was to show us to ourselves.

PRIDE OF WORK

For centuries artists have used the land to make heroes of those who toil at it. In Part I we saw how artists depict nature. We also saw how artists show the human struggle for survival against the threats of nature. In many other works we have seen how artists paint people working the land or traveling through a landscape. These pictures show the human being at one with nature, working in harmony with the natural elements, enjoying them, and sharing them. We will now look at four different interpretations of people as tillers of the soil.

First, look at the picture *The Fall of Icarus*. It was painted by Pieter Brueghel, the Elder in 1564. You saw another work by Brueghel on page 71 in Part I of this book. The title of this painting comes from Greek mythology. It is the story of Daedalus and his son Icarus. In the story Daedalus and his son are trying to escape from the King of Crete. Daedalus makes wings out of wax and feathers so he and Icarus can fly away. Although Daedalus warns Icarus not to fly too high, the boy gets too close to the sun. The wax melts and he falls into the sea.

How does Brueghel show this extraordinary event? Look again at the painting. Can you find Icarus? if you are looking out to the sky and distant sea, you are looking too far. Look down. Do you see two legs and a splash between the

Figure 168A. *The Fall of Icarus* **by Pieter Brueghel, the Elder, painted around 1564.**

ship and the shore? That is Icarus. Now look at the other people in the painting. How do they respond?

Such a momentous event had no meaning for those who must till the land. At the center of the painting is the plowman at his plow. Notice how Brueghel painted thick furrows of soil to depict the heavy workload. Below, the shepherd tends his sheep, more concerned about their safety than about a splash in the sea. Even the wind fills the sail of the ship and carries it beyond the fallen Icarus. In this painting, Brueghel is showing us that these people do not care about the disaster that has befallen Icarus. They do not have time for such things. Daedalus, the one person who would care, is not included in this scene.

The characters in Brueghel's masterpiece come from a poem by the ancient Roman poet Ovid. Read how Ovid described the fall of Icarus.

Far off, far down some fisherman is watching
as the rod dips and trembles over the water.
Some shepherd rests his weight upon his crook
Some plowman on the handles of a plow
All look up in absolute amazement
at those airborne above,
On the mirror smooth sea.

Is this what Brueghel has painted? No, not at all.
Brueghel deliberately chose to paint this amazing event and
show that no one stopped work to notice it. Although
Brueghel used Ovid's characters, he was really portraying
something else. Brueghel was portraying the spirit of a
proverb, or saying, popular among the hardworking people
of Flanders. That proverb is: "No plow comes to rest because
a man dies."

Figure 168B. A detail of Brueghel's painting.

Brueghel painted *The Fall of Icarus* in the 1500s. Hundreds of years later, in the 1900s, it inspired a poet, W. H. Auden, to write a famous poem. Part of that poem, "Museé des Beaux Arts," is printed here.

About suffering they were never wrong,
The Old Masters: how well they understood
Its human position; how it takes place
While someone else is eating or opening a window or just
walking dully along; . . .

In Brueghel's *Icarus*, for instance: how everything turns away

Quite leisurely from the disaster; the plowman may
Have heard the splash, the forsaken cry,
But for him it was not an important failure; the sun shone

As it had to on the white legs disappearing into the green
Water; and the expensive delicate ship that must have seen
Something amazing, a boy falling out of the sky,
Had somewhere to get to and sailed calmly on.

W. H. Auden must have studied Brueghel's painting very carefully. Brueghel must have studied Ovid's poem. So for two thousand years the story of Icarus has been a source of inspiration. Although the poets and the artist lived hundreds of years apart, each in his own way borrowed and integrated the idea of man and his work.

In 1850, the French artist Jean Francois Millet (pronounced *me-lay*) painted a picture called *The Sower*. It was considered a revolutionary painting. Before that time, hardworking peasants had never been considered a worthy subject for French art.

Millet's picture gave the peasant the importance and dignity of a king. Notice how the artist designed the painting to tell the story. Night is falling. Dark shadows stretch across the field, and the sky darkens the world. Still, the sower strides on in his majestic way. He pays no attention to the time of day or the hungry crows following him. This man has a life-giving bond with the earth. It is the seeds that he sows on the ground that will bring bread to the table. The painting shows the peasant's attachment to the land and the sweat, toil, and pride of his work.

**Figure 169. Millet's *The Sower* shows his consideration of the
common people as subjects worthy for painting.**

Millet explained his painting with these words: "'Thou
shalt live by the sweat of the brow' was written centuries
ago and the destiny of man will never change."

Many critics of the time thought that Millet was trying to
stir up the peasants. In 1789 (sixty-one years earlier), the
French Revolution had promised "liberty, equality, frater-
nity" for everyone. To some people Millet's painting suggested that the hard lot of the peasant had not improved.
Does Millet's giant of a man suggest that the peasants rise
up and revolt? Is his hand swinging out to cast the seeds of
discontent? What do you think?

One reason the public did not like Millet's paintings was
their *realism*. The French public did not mind seeing happy,
carefree peasants. People objected to realism because it was
not always pretty. They did not want to be reminded of hard

work, weary bones, and mud and dirt. For many people it recalled a world they had moved to the city to get away from. These people found it threatening to remember their country upbringing.

Millet was one of a growing group of artists called "social realists." These artists were so named because they painted pictures about the hardships of life. They showed work and suffering instead of happy, sentimental times. Although these artists showed everyday activities, they were different from genre painters. They did not just show people doing simple tasks such as sewing or reading letters. Instead, they showed that work and life could be difficult and unpleasant. This was when "genre" began to turn into social realism.

In the next two paintings, by the modern Mexican artist Diego Rivera, we will see another form of social realism. The murals of Diego Rivera dramatize the history, dignity, toil, and sweat of Mexican peasants and laborers. His murals adorn the walls of public buildings throughout Mexico City. The huge images celebrate the daily life of the peasants on the land and the workers in the factories. Two of his best murals are *The Market* and *The Sugar Refiners*.

In *The Market* the people show character, dignity, and hope. They bring their pineapples, pottery jugs, and crates of fruit from their land to sell in the city. Like Millet's sower, they are workers of the soil, close to the land.

In *The Sugar Refiners*, Rivera's workers move in their space to the rhythm of their work. *The Sugar Refiners* is a ballet of lines and shapes describing backbreaking work and human endurance.

Rivera's murals are a combination of styles from modern art and the ancient tradition of wall painting. In earlier centuries, murals showed dramas taken from the Bible, myths, or a country's history. The muralist was an artisan who told stories with pictures. They were simple to understand and gave inspiration to everyone. Uneducated people could read them in place of books.

In the case of Diego Rivera, mural painting presented a problem and a challenge. In his early career, Diego Rivera lived in Europe and painted in a modern style. When he began to discover his own country's history and the condition of the Mexican worker, he left Europe and returned to Mexico. His murals are an attempt to bring art to all the people, and to give to them a pride in their heritage through art.

The paintings of Brueghel and Millet show us how the artist glorified work in an agricultural world. With the

Figure 170. *The Market*, a mural by Mexican artist Diego Rivera (1886–1957).

Figure 171. *The Sugar Refiners*, also by Diego Rivera, shows people hard at work.

Figure 172. *Miners' Wives* by Ben Shahn expresses the sometimes grim life in a mining town. 1948.

work of Rivera, we also find an agricultural people leaving the land and working in the city. But the marketplace and the sugar refinery still draw their raw materials from nature.

The next painting shows still another kind of labor, and another kind of struggle with nature. This painting, by Ben Shahn, is called *Miners' Wives*. You looked at other Ben Shahn paintings in Unit 5.

In this painting we see the miners through their wives. What is this woman thinking? What is she feeling, this aging tired woman staring out at us? An old grandmother sits with the child. The painting does not show the workers, but the wives of the workers, the women wait and grow up waiting for their fathers and husbands and sons who go into the mines and factories. Day in and day out at home, in the stores, enclosed in backyards under factory smoke, they work and wait, holding their families together. The painting is Ben Shahn's tribute. He doesn't show us the miners, he shows us the bleakness and suffering of their lives.

Notice the coat hanging on the red brick wall. Perhaps it belongs to the father who is not there. Who are the two men walking away? Have they been there to tell this woman about trouble at the mine? What does the woman's expression show? Is it disbelief? The painting tells much in its use of stark, flat shapes. *Miners' Wives* is yet another example of social realism.

This section began with Brueghel's *Icarus*. In the time when Brueghel lived, people were one with nature in an agricultural society. To them, life and death were all part of the same grand scheme. Today, we live in an industrial society where people reap, but do not sow. The works of Millet, Rivera, and Shahn show how these artists have noted the changes. They also show how much the artists care if farmers break their backs plowing fields, if people leave their land to work in sugar refineries, if families of coal miners weep when disaster strikes.

In their own ways, artists are saying "I care ... I care, and I want you to care."

Summary Questions

1. How did Pieter Brueghel use the *Fall of Icarus* to convey the peasants' attitude toward work?

2. Why was Jean Francois Millet's painting *The Sower* considered revolutionary?

3. Who were the "Social Realists"?

4. Why did people object to realism in the 1800's?

5. On what surfaces did Diego Rivera paint his pictures?

6. What was Rivera attempting to do with his art?

7. Who are the coal miners in Ben Shahn's painting?

8. How has the artist's vision of people who work changed over the centuries?

ACTIVITIES

1 and 2. Environment: Natural/Man-made There are two kinds of environments: natural and man-made. Both are affected by man. How many times have you seen trash left on the streets or observed discarded rubbish on the highways? Of course, you have seen state highway signs informing everyone of their responsibility to see how people adversely affect the natural environment.

But what about the man-made environment? How does man affect it? First of all, someone had to design and build the man-made environment. New buildings, parks, shopping centers, and highways usually look very nice when completed, but as time goes by people forget their responsibilities toward the man-made environment.

Look around your community and select three places in the man-made environment that have a special meaning to people. Make a sketch of how they may have looked when first completed. What has happened to them? Are they as nice and well-kept now as when they were new? Has "man" left trash around to detract from the original appearance? Were they poorly planned in the first place? (For example, have people cut across the grass in the park because the sidewalks are not convenient?)

Consider yourself a city planner (with an unlimited budget). Re-do your sketch, making changes to make that special place easier to use, more fun to be in, or more beautiful. You may change the placement of existing objects, add or remove objects, and change the colors.

3. Collecting Art   Start an art collection of your own. Reproductions of famous art works are available in magazines and Sunday newspaper sections on the arts. Many can be purchased in postcard size from museums. Your collection may be limited to one artist, one style, one period, or, it could cover a larger range. Place your reproductions in a notebook. Make notes about the artists, media, period, style.

Some libraries loan out art reproductions. If your library does, you could borrow one and hang it in your room for several weeks.

4. Knowing About Art   You can learn to recognize that a work was created by a specific artist even though you may never have seen it before. Look at the ten works of art displayed on the board. Can you pick out those that were done by Grant Wood? Consider such clues as subject matter, use of light and color, size of objects, mood. Tell the class why you think all three of the ones you picked were painted by Wood.

5. Knowing About Art: Timeline   Works of art may be organized in order of the time period in which they were created. With some practice and discussions about characteristics of work made in different periods of time, you can make fairly accurate estimates of the time period.

The following list indicates the route you might take in investigating or unraveling the puzzle of the time periods of selected works of art. A good art dictionary will be of great help.

(a) What style is the work?
(b) What is the material or medium used?
(c) How long has that particular material been available to artists?
(d) If the piece is a painting, what is it painted on? Wood? Canvas? Cardboard? Paper? If the piece is a sculpture, is it stone? Wood? Metal? Fiberglass?
(e) What is the subject matter?
(f) What style of clothing are the figures wearing?

Cut out an oaktag strip that is one yard long and 5 inches high. Draw the timeline on it beginning with 1300 A.D. and moving to the present. The timeline can be folded in 1-foot sections for easy storage. Each time you see and read about a work of art, try to use the clues above to pinpoint when the work was done. Write its name and artist at the correct point on the line.

6. Art Exhibition Work as a group to set up a class exhibit of artwork. Pretend that you work at a museum and are planning an exhibition of artwork by artists in the area. The following are some things to think about:

(a) Which artists in the community are you going to show? Will it be an exhibit of one artist or a group show?

(b) Determine the dates for the show.

(c) Who will organize the exhibition and hang the work? Where will the work be exhibited?

(d) Who will write the press release? Who will be invited?

(e) Who will design a catalog?

(f) Who will plan a preview?

Make detailed lists of all the tasks to be done and plan a schedule.

7. Art Books Select one of the following themes to explore in art books and magazines.

• social (work day, labor force, etc.)
• ceremonial (holidays, rituals)
• historical (battles, explorations)

Choose art books or magazines from the library and find examples of your theme. Make notes on 3 x 5-inch cards about the examples you found. Describe how the artist treated each work. Be sure to note the source, page number, name of the artist, and title of the work. Describe the art qualities in each work. Also describe what clues each work gives to the kind of life that people lived at the time.

THE ART MUSEUM EXPERIENCE

Soon after the American Revolution, Charles Willson Peale founded America's first art museum in Philadelphia. Peale was famous for his portraits of George Washington. He was an inventor-scientist and a man interested in practically everything. In his painting *The Artist in His Museum* he is standing in front of a curtain near some stuffed birds. Inside, spectators look at boxes of stuffed animals, insects, and fish beneath portraits of American patriots.

A story about Peale's museum illustrates the possibilities of such institutions. According to the story, two rival Indian chiefs came to visit the museum at the same time. These two men had met before only on the field of battle. They were sworn enemies. Would there be trouble in the museum? Not at all. Interpreters explained the exhibits to the visitors. As the two chiefs marveled at the wonders of art and science, they came to the same conclusion: The abilities of human beings were so great, wouldn't it be better to work together in peace than apart as enemies? So these men buried the hatchet and became brothers.

What is the purpose of this story? First, museums do reflect the achievements of people. And second, these particular visitors had what is known as a museum experience.

Figure 173. *The Artist in His Museum* by Charles Willson Peale (1824).

There is a difference between a visit and an experience. When you merely visit a museum, you look at art but don't really see it. A museum experience can change your life because it changes your understanding of something.

What happens when you enter an art museum? Suddenly you are in front of several paintings on the walls or art objects on the floor. On the first visit, time does not permit you to see everything. So you find a painting you like and stay with it. Why do you like this particular work? It may take some time before you can answer that question. Over a period of time you will select favorite works and from looking, thinking, and discussing, you will understand what makes them so appealing to you.

Perhaps you have selected with the class or your teacher one particular work to examine. If you have previously seen a copy of this work, you can immediately tell the difference. People can make very good copies of art works, and we can learn much from them. Still, there is no substitute for the original colors of a painting or textures of a sculpture. This is the most important reason to visit a museum, but it is only the beginning.

An art museum is a living record of the past and present. You may go to a museum to see a great painting that is considered by many to be a masterpiece. You may also visit museums to see many other kinds of art. All have their own beauty, power, and message.

Figure 174. The Temple of Dendur from ancient Egypt now stands at the Metropolitan Museum of Art in New York City.

Figure 175. Armor for man and horse from medieval Europe was a symbol of the age of chivalry.

Look at the reproductions of museum pieces. The first is an Egyptian temple; the second, medieval armor; the third, is an evening gown made by the House of Worth. These are all important works of art from our earliest history to the present time. Each piece expresses values, ideals, and beliefs of different civilizations. As we study them, we come closer to our past and ourselves—who we were and what we are. In the art objects of the past we relive our history. In contemporary art we come to see ourselves through the genius of living artists. The art of the past restores human memory. The art of the present offers visions of the future.

**Figure 176. An evening
gown by the House
of Worth on display
at a museum.**

The museum experience can change your life—in how you
see yourself or how you look at the world. For example, as
you look at the art objects from everyday life (the dress , the
armor) the question arises: Which objects in your life will
someday be in a museum—and why? Could you find an
object such as a favorite chair, cup, or bike and look at it
through the eyes of an artist? Winslow Homer taught us
how to see colors. Now try looking at your own room as if it
were a painting. Find in your own community a house with
a Gothic shape or an old automobile. From your museum
experience could you determine what those relics of the past
have to do with you? That's the challenge—because once
you have been to the museum, you can have the museum
experience anywhere. For art is everywhere.

P A R T

III

THE ARTIST
AS STUDENT

UNIT 7

THE STUDENT AS ARTIST

In this book you have learned about the elements and principles of design. You have seen how many different artists use these in their work. As an art student, you have been learning how to use them too.

On the following pages you will find the work of other students who have been learning to apply the elements and principles in a variety of mediums. Studying the work of others can help give you new ideas and insights about what you yourself are doing. As a student, you can never find out too much!

In a way all artists are students. That is because an artist is always learning, experimenting, and looking for new ways to express things. Not every attempt is successful, but every attempt is important for it shows that the artist/student is still growing, still seeking the endless possibilities of visual communication.

Art A and B

The two designs above use many of the same forms and colors, yet the student artists have achieved very different results. What effect does the ragged black line have around one design? How does it compare to the mood of the other design?

Art A.

Art B.

Art C

In this work the students experimented with color and shape to execute their compositions. Notice how the form is simplified and slightly abstracted. What elements create movement in the paintings below?

Art C.

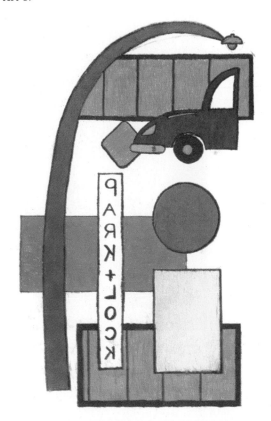

Art E and F

Which of these compositions has more movement? More texture and pattern? How does the repetition of color affect the design of each work?

Art E.

Art F.

Art G and H

How do the birds in each of these paintings differ? Why is green important to the unity of design of the painting on the left? Both students included dark lines in their compositions. How does the function of these lines differ?

Art H.

Art G.

Art I

Notice how this student has used soft color to achieve a warm, pleasant feeling. What season do you think it is? What kind of perspective has this student used?

Art I.

Art J and K

How many different kinds of lines has the student created with a brush? How do the lines add to the whimsy of this work? The student who made the print used line in another way. Notice how the lines in the print define shapes and forms.

Art J.

Art K.

Art L

By overlapping the birds, this student has attempted to show depth in space. How has the student created emphasis in this work?

Art L.

Art M and N

Both of these works are collages. Notice that similar materials were used. Which collage has the greater movement? How did the student create values of tone?

Art M.

Art N.

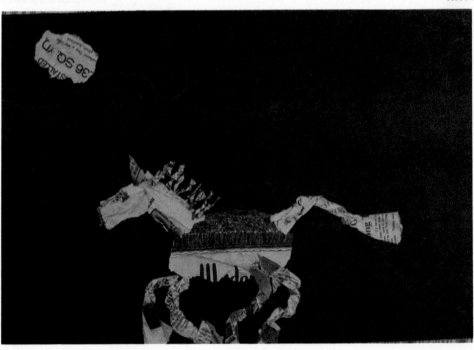

Art O, P, and Q

Which of these sculptures is the most abstract? Which artists repeated forms and colors to create an effect?

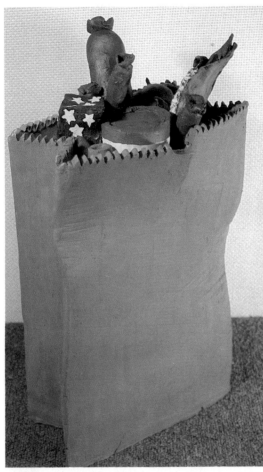

Art O.

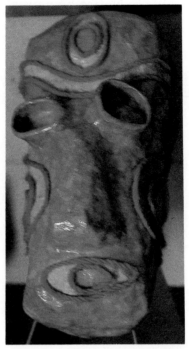

Art P.

Art Q.

Art R and S

Notice how proudly this lion stands! The artist used the lion's tail to help balance its puffed up chest.

Using just wire, a student created this graceful figure. Notice how much movement it has. What forms are repeated?

Art R.

Art S.

Art T and U

The student artists who made these pots used simple shapes and clean lines to create beautiful pottery.

Art T.

Art U.

Art V and W

In the photograph above a student's camera captured the texture of a rusty dashboard. Notice how the photographer used the steering wheel to frame the focal point of the picture. Shadow and light help create a stark contrast in the photograph of the bird. Notice how each part of this photograph is an important form.

Art V.

Art W.

GLOSSARY

Apex The uppermost point, such as of a triangle or mountain.

Artisan A skilled worker who painted images and decorations on walls. Today an artisan is a person such as a carpenter, tailor, or plumber.

Art Nouveau (ahr noo–voh´) French "new art." A style of decoration originating in United States in the 1880's and extending to Europe in the 1890's to the 1900's. A graceful, rhythmic design based on plant and natural forms using curves, especially in architecture, interior decoration, furniture, and crafts.

Arts and Crafts Movement Developed in England mainly by William Morris (1834-96) as a revolt against an increasingly industrialized society. He produced wallpapers, furniture, tapestries, stained-glass windows, book designs, and printing from his own private press.

Artist A person who makes art, usually used for visual artists but also applies to poets and performing artists, such as dancers, musicians, and actors.

Balance In art, a position of equilibrium of all the elements. There are three types: formal or symmetrical, informal or asymmetrical, and radial balance.

Bas-relief (bah-ree-leef´) (see *Relief Sculpture*)

Baseline The line at the bottom of a drawing or painting representing the ground or floor, especially in artwork by children in kindergarten or first grade.

Ceramic A term applied to objects made from baked or fired caly, earthernware or porcelain, and pottery. Usually cups, bowls, and pots, but may also be ceramic sculpture such as figurines or glazed statues.

Collage Pieces of pictures, and materials cut and pasted together in a design or new picture. *(See Photo Montage)*

Color An element of design that gives the sensation of hue, tone, or shade produced through the reflection of light by the eye. The primary colors are: red, yellow, and blue; the secondary ones are: orange, green, and violet.

Conceptualized Art A drawing made from the imagination or memory in which the artist depicts what he or she knows about a thing instead of what is seen by looking at it.

Contrast A principle of design in which the artist chooses a variety of colors, textures, and patterns to add interest to a work.

Cosmos An orderly, systematic, and harmonious universe.

Design Composition A preliminary sketch or outline showing the main features of an artwork.

Diadem A crown or royal headband.

Dimension A measurement in one direction. The four dimensions are height, width, depth, and time.

Emphasis A principle of design in which the artist makes one aspect of a work more important than another by making it dominant.

Engraving A reproduction process in which the design is cut directly into the surface of a plate by pointed steel tool called a burin, and the ink is rubbed into the incised lines. It is then printed under heavy pressure.

Etching A method of engraving in which the design is eaten into a copper plate coated with acid. A steel needlelike pen is used by the artist.

Foreshortening The drawing of single objects or people in perspective, so that they look shorter than they really are.

Form The shape and structure of something as distinguished from its material.

French Revolution The revolution in France (1789-1799) that followed and was influenced by the American Revolution. Louis XVI and Marie Antoinette were deposed by their subjects.

Genre Painting that shows realistic scenes or events from everyday life.

Gothic Shape A shape characterized by pointed arches (to develop greater height), especially in cathedrals. It began in northern France and spread throughout Europe during the twelfth through sixteenth centuries.

Graphic Arts The arts of decoration, advertising, book and magazine illustration, cartoons, and signs for commercial purposes. (See *Printmaking*)

Graphite A soft black lustrous carbon that is used in lead pencils.

Guild A medieval association of merchants or craftsmen with similar professional interests and crafts skills.

Illusion The use of perspective and foreshortening to fool the eye into believing that what is painted is real. (See *Foreshortening*)

Industrial Revolution In the late 1800's a rapid change in an economy, in England particularly, marked by power-driven machinery and the growth of factories.

Interpretation The explanation or meaning of things.

Landscape Painting A work of art that depicts the natural environment—the ocean, mountains, flowers, trees.

Lapis Lazuli (*lap´-is laz´-u-lee*) A semiprecious stone of a rich azure blue worn by the Inca kings of Peru and pharoahs of Egypt.

Line That which defines and encloses a space. It may be two-dimensional (pen on paper), three-dimensional (wood), or implied (the edge of an object).

Lithograph A method of surface printing from stone. The design is drawn on the flat surface of a slab of special limestone with a greasy ink or crayon. A sheet of paper is placed on the stone and passed through a lithographic press.

Medium The material used by an artist to apply pigments and colors to a surface, such as linseed oil, water, acrylic, or wax. The substance in which a sculptor chooses to create an image such as metal, wood, or marble, or in which a craftsperson chooses to create an article such as clay, enamel, mosaic, or fabrics.

Middle Ages The period of European history from about A.D. 500 to around 1500.

Movement A principle of design in which the artist uses lines, colors, values, textures, forms and space to direct the eye of the viewer from one part of the picture to another.

Mural Painting A large painting (usually) done directly on a wall.

Narrative Painting A painting that tells a story.

Neolithic Period The latest period of the Stone Age characterized by polished stone implements. (c. 3000-1600 B.C.)

One-Point Perspective A technique for representing depth by showing an object from one point of view, for example, showing only one side or one surface to the viewer; distant objects recede to a point on the horizon or eye-level line.

Perspective A technique by which artists in the Western European tradition from the Italian Renaissance to the present depict three-dimensional space (depth) on a two-dimensional surface.

Photo Montage A collage made only of parts of photographs and pictures cut and pasted together. (See *Collage*)

Photography The art or technique of producing images on a sensitized film by the action of light. It came into general use in 1839.

Pigment A powdered substance that adds a color to other materials such as paints, inks, or plastics.

Points of View The standpoints from which an artist draws or paints his or her subject matter (view, scene, still life, portrait, etc.)

Portrait A work of art featuring a person's face or full figure. It can include families as well.

Post-Impressionism A style of art that directly followed Impressionism. It stressed the importance of the subject, color, or expressionism. Cézanne and Van Gogh were some of its most important artists.

Principles of Design The rules an artist follows in the visual arts. Most often they are: balance, emphasis, movement, variety, proportion, and unity.

Printmaking The process of making an image which can be printed and repeated several times by stamping, pressing, or squeezing paint through a stenciled shape; usually designated by the type of medium used, i.e., wood, linoleum, stone, or silkscreen.

Proportion A term used to mean that one part of an image or design is in relationship to, or in balance with, another part of the image or design, such as having different parts of the human body in proportion with other parts, or one color or shape not being out of balance with another shape or color.

Radial Balance   A design based on a circle with its features spreading out from a central point.

Realism   A style of art that depicts objects, people, and events as they really are, instead of idealistically or romantically.

Relief Sculpture   A sculpture that is not free standing. It has a background, and is three-dimensional. It is usually placed on a wall. Relief sculpture can be sunk or raised. Sometimes called bas-relief.

Sculpture   The art of creating forms in three dimensions by carving, construction, or modeling.

Serigraph   See *Silkscreen*.

Shaman   A priest who uses magic to cure the sick, divine the hidden, and control events.

Shang Dynasty   In China, a period (1600-1027 B.C.) that developed a rich Bronze Age culture and the first written documents. The Shang Dynasty of 30 kings practiced fraternal succession and were masters of the Yellow River plain in China.

Shape   An element of design where one end of a line meets the other end of a line to create a closed space. It can be regular (geometrical) or irregular (natural).

Silkscreen   A screen made of fine silk stretched on a frame and treated to make a stenciled image that is created by squeezing paint through the untreated areas. The prints made by silkscreen are also called serigraphs.

Social Realism   A movement in art depicting life with its hardships and suffering. It began with Courbet and includes Millet.

Space   As an element in design, space is the void or area around solid and flat shapes. In art this relationship is sometimes referred to as negative and positive space.

Spectrum   The band of colors caused when a beam of light is passed through a prism (a triangular piece of glass). The colors follow the same sequence (red, orange, yellow, green, blue, and violet) as seen in a rainbow.

Technique   A means to express oneself through working with materials.

Tactile Surface   Relating to the sense of touch.

Tempera Painting   A process of painting in which egg yolk and varnishes are used as a binder. It was the most common technique used until the late 1400's, when it was replaced with linseed and other oils.

Texture   An element of design that is experienced through a sense of touch, such as actual (natural and invented) or rough and smooth, hard and soft. Simulated textures are printed or drawn on a smooth surface to appear rough or smooth, hard or soft.

Three-Dimensional   Having height, depth, and width. A sculpture has three dimension; a picture of a sculpture has only two dimensions. (See *Relief Sculpture*)

Two-Dimensional   Having height and width, but lacking depth. A painting or print has two dimensions. (See *Relief Sculpture*)

Unity   A principle of design that identifies when all the other principles and elements of a design look or work well together to give a single statement or image, all of the same style. Nothing appears out of place or inconsistent with the whole.

Value   A term used to identify or define the relative lightness, greyness, or darkness of a color, picture, or design; also used to distinguish the range of white to gret to black in colorless images and designs.

Visual Arts   The arts as seen in still forms such as drawing, painting, sculpture, photography, and film, rather than heard such as music or watched such as dance and drama. As a series of still images seen in rapid sequence, film is considered a Visual Art.

Woodcut   The oldest technique for making prints. It is a relief process done on a smooth, flat, wood surface, The design is cut away with a knife, then inked and pressed by hand or a press onto a sheet of paper. The result is an impression in reverse of the original design.

Index and Pronunciation Guide

Boldface page numbers indicate location of illustrations.